SUPER
LITTLE GIANT BOOK™ OF
SECRET CODES

SUPER
LITTLE GIANT BOOK™ OF
SECRET CODES

DAVID LAMBERT
& THE DIAGRAM GROUP

Sterling Publishing Co., Inc.
New York

Library of Congress Cataloging-in-Publication Data Available

10 9 8 7 6 5 4 3 2 1

Published in 2007 by Sterling Publishing Co., Inc.
387 Park Avenue South, New York, N.Y. 10016

Created by Diagram Visual Information Limited
195 Kentish Town Road, London, NW5 2JU, England

© 2007 Diagram Visual Information Limited

Distributed in Canada by Sterling Publishing
c/o Canadian Manda Group, 165 Dufferin Street,
Toronto, Ontario, Canada M6K 3H6

Written by	Bruce Robertson
Production	Richard Hummerstone
Design	Anthony Atherton, Lee Lawrence, Philip Richardson
Picture research	Neil McKenna, Patricia Robertson
Artist	Pavel Kostal
Code checker	Ben Oliver

Sterling ISBN-13: 978-1-4027-3739-8
       ISBN 10: 1-4027-3739-4

For information about custom editions, special sales, premium and
corporate purchases, please contact Sterling Special Sales Department
on 800-805-5489 or specialsales@sterlingpub.com.

INTRODUCTION

* Learning ways of hiding messages to your friends can be fun!
* Code-making is a very old skill and easy to learn.
* Hundreds of years before Christ, the Greeks used a secret method of communicating that you will learn.
* The Romans, medieval monks, Leonardo da Vinci, and ambassadors to the Court of the English Queen Elizabeth I also used these codes.
* You will learn ways of sending messages used by Native Americans, sailors, racing car drivers, and pilots in distress.
* In wartime, code-makers have played a key role in securing victories: you too will learn codes from the War of Independence, the Civil War, and World Wars I and II.

The book contains three basic methods of creating codes.
* By *transposition*: that's mixing the letters of your code.
* By *substitution*: that's replacing letters with numbers or symbols.
* By *signs and signals*: that's using flags or other devices to represent the letters or words.

WELCOME TO THE WORLD OF SECRET CODES

CONTENTS

162 3 SIGNS, SIGNALS, AND SYMBOLS

272 LAST WORDS

10

TEST YOUR CODE SKILLS

* Many of the codes in this book begin with a message using the code.
* Once you have read the method used, try to decode the message.
* Be careful – errors and tricks have been included in the messages!

IVRV   KYZJ   DVJJRXV

90110-33129-1372

20-166220-109228

TRANSPOSITION CIPHERS

y w j u k p

P d e o

A **transposition cipher** is a way of coding a message where the character positions are changed, but the characters themselves stay the same.

At times the cipher you receive is a pure transpositional cipher.

nawz

ykzə

See pages 20–21 to work it out!

Or it may be a cross between transpositional and substitution ciphers.

In both cases you will have to figure it out using your wits and the information you share with your friends and accomplices.

MIND THE GAP

ICANREADTHISMESSAGE

A thousand years before the invention of printing, Irish monks created books by having scribes copy from earlier manuscripts. They laboriously wrote out the entire text to produce a duplicate.

To speed production, one scribe read the manuscript out very slowly while two or more wrote down what he said.

In ancient Egyptian, Hebrew, Greek, and Latin texts, the letters that make up the words are individual characters with no spaces between the groups:

HOWTEXTAPPEAREDTOROMANREADERS

To enable readers to read out whole words and not individual letters, they read aloud each word, which was then copied as it was pronounced.

It seems the Irish invented words by accidentally inserting gaps between the rows of letters.

A Latin text from AD 510 without word breaks.

A passage from the Book of Kells *created by Irish scribes with word gaps in the late 8th century AD.*

PLOW WRITING

The Ancient Greeks wrote their texts using a style they called *boustrophedon,* which means "turning like an ox when plowing." They had no spaces between words, and alternate lines were written backward across the page. This meant they could write the letters of their alphabet both backward and forward.

READ THE LINES IN ALTERNATE
DIRECTIONS ONE FROM LEFT
TO RIGHT THE NEXT FROM RIGHT

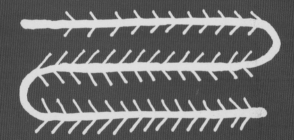

Can you write out the lines of the text above in this style?

QUICK MESSAGE

IC AN RE AD

EGASSEM SIH

EGA SSE MSI

CI NA ER DA HT

You can easily turn your message into a code by changing the order of the letters, by moving the word spaces, or by both.

In *random reverse* you write down the message backward, then break it into different numbers of groups:

a) EGASSEM SIHT DAER NAC I

CODES

TH IS ME SS AG E

T DAER NAC I

HTD AERN ACI

I EM SS GA E

b) EGA SSE MSI HTD AERN ACI

In *bi-reverse* you write down your message in reverse, then break the message into groups of two, then write each group backward:

IC AN RE AD TH IS ME SS AG E
CI NA ER DA HT SI EM SS GA E

DISPLACEMENT CODES

This method is very simple as it only requires you to write out the alphabet with even spacing, then repeat it below, this time starting below a selected letter.

Your secret message will then be in the same order as your true message, but encoded.

When you write out your alphabet, take care to space each letter apart equally,

A B C D E F G H I J K
w x y z a b c d e f g

This code is a displacement from A to W. You can choose any letter to start the new row.

even though the letters *I* and *J* are narrower than *M* and *W*. This even spacing is to ensure that when you move the second alphabet forward, each letter remains directly below another.

Begin writing your coded message with the letter representing *A* so the person you are sending it to can write out the second alphabet under *A*, beginning with *W*. You could tell your friend to begin their displacement with the initial letter of their first name. In this example, William.

L M N O P Q R S T U V
h i j k l m n o p q r
        W X Y Z
        s t u v

ANAGRAMS

The ciphers on the previous pages are transposition ciphers. This is basically a method in which the letters of a message are rearranged without actually replacing a word's letters with other letters, numbers, or symbols. **Anagrams**, which became popular in the 17th century, are a well-known example of transposition technique. Astronomers such as Galileo and Johannes Kepler were among the first to use this technique.

Anagrams rearrange the letters of a single word, creating new words in the process. For instance, the word "cat" becomes "act," the word "war" becomes "raw," etc.

The history of this technique is not clear. It may have begun when ancient scribes chose to rearrange the characters of, for instance, their ruler's name for security or ritual purposes.

Spies often rearranged the letters of their names to use as a password.

You could try re-arranging the letters of your name to form another word.

Mr Pelker can be made from Kepler (top right), Mr Logiale from Galileo (below right).

Can you unscramble these anagrams?
They are the names of people mentioned
in this book.

1 A BLINDED CORNET

2 BARMY MALE JESTER

3 A RANCID DEVON OIL

4 JANE OFFERS MOTHS

5 ALSO SEE MR MU

6 IN JINKS HOWL

RAT BILE (7)

A RICH ELVES MINT (8)

PLACED EACH UP (9)

HEH SMELLS CROOK (10)

KEY WORD CODES

These are transposition ciphers created by swapping the letters of your message with the matching letters in a key word alphabet. You can exchange coded messages with a friend who knows the key word.

To make a coded message:
• Write out the alphabet.
• Write out your key word alphabet below.
• Select the letters of your message from

A	B	C	D	E	F	G	H	I	J	K	L	M
H	A	R	L	E	Q	U	I	N	B	C	D	

the top row and replace them with letters from the lower row.

You begin with a key word or phrase in which no letter is repeated and continue alphabetically, omitting the letters of your key word as you go.

The lower line then becomes your alphabet for creating coded messages. You could use your own name as your key word.

| O | P | Q | R | S | T | U | V | W | X | Y | Z |
| J | K | M | O | P | S | T | V | W | X | Y | Z |

5B UTI MSTR

A	B	C	D	E	F	G	H	I	J	K	L	M
T	H	U	R	S	D	A	Y	B	C	E	F	G

The key word used by you and your friend can be changed daily. For example, you could use each day of the week starting with Sunday – so start each message with a number representing the day.

A	B	C	D	E	F	G	H	I	J	K	L	M
M	O	N	O	A	Y	B	C	E	F	G	H	I

2E NMJ QAMD

N	O	P	Q	R	S	T	U	V	W	X	Y	Z
I	J	K	L	M	N	O	P	Q	V	W	X	Z

Your friend knows the fifth day is Thursday so he writes that day first followed by the other letters of the alphabet. The message at the bottom is the same but written on a Monday.

N	O	P	Q	R	S	T	U	V	W	X	Y	Z
J	K	L	P	Q	R	S	T	U	V	W	X	Z

SCER IARRMBA

GEOMETRIC CIPHERS

A *geometric cipher* is a type of transposition cipher. A geometric design, known as a matrix (array or grid), is filled out with the *plaintext* – the actual message you want to encode. If you move in a planned direction – up or down each column – a different order of the letters results. A key you share with your friends defines the size and direction of the route.

Simple geometric forms involve very basic ways of rearranging letters. For example, the words

I CAN READ THIS MESSAGE

can be written downwards in a stack of spaces. To choose a grid divide the letters in your message into two or three columns

The ciphertext is drawn from the horizontal pairs to create the cryptogram:

II CS AM NE RS ES AA DG TE H

You can send your code reading off each two-letter group, or as written at the top of the page opposite in groups of three.

IE IS CA SA AD

IR TM AC EH EG

I	D	S
C	T	S
A	H	A
N	I	G
R	S	E
E	M	
A	E	

I	E	I	S
C	A	S	A
A	D	M	G
N	T	E	E
R	H	S	

IG RS EEMA E

MG NT EE RH S

AA IS EN DS S

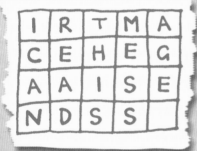

This message has been written on three, four, and five unit-wide grids. You would tell your friends

3 by 7
4 by 5
5 by 4

Then the codes above were set in pairs.

ciex ismx rdax

BOXED CODES

You can write another transposition cipher
devised by using a grid of 4 x 6 squares, a
key word, and a route on the grid for your
message.

- The message can be up to 24 letters long.
- Your key word can be any word of four
  or six letters in which none of the letters
  appears more than once.
- The route is the direction on the grid in
  which you write out your message. This
  is written under or beside your key
  word. If there are fewer than 24 letters in
  your message fill the spaces with the
  letter X. On pages 36 and 37 are six
     examples of routes you could choose.

ntsx ahsx eage

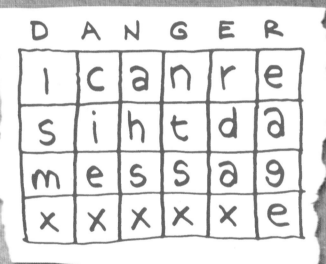

D	A	N	G	E	R
I	c	a	n	r	e
s	i	h	t	d	a
m	e	s	s	a	g
x	x	x	x	x	e

This is the message to be sent written out
using the DANGER grid on page 37.

METHOD

A	B	C	D	E	F
G	H	I	J	K	L
M	N	O	P	Q	R
S	T	U	V	W	X

ACTION

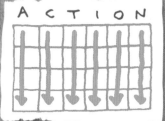

A	E	I	M	Q	U
B	F	J	N	R	V
C	G	K	O	S	W
D	H	L	P	T	X

SHADOW

A	P	O	N	M	L
B	Q	X	W	V	K
C	R	S	T	U	J
D	E	F	G	H	I

DANGER

A	B	C	D	E	F
L	K	J	I	H	G
M	N	O	P	Q	R
X	W	V	U	T	S

SPIDER

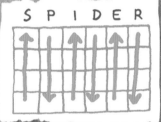

D	E	I	P	Q	X
C	F	J	O	R	W
B	G	K	N	S	V
A	H	L	M	T	U

VICTIM

F	E	D	C	B	A
G	T	S	R	Q	P
H	U	V	W	X	O
I	J	K	L	M	N

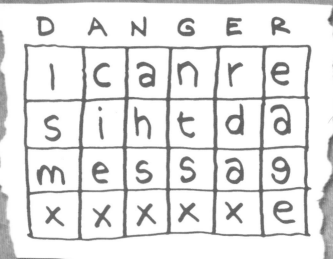

After you have written your message on the grid in the pattern you selected (DANGER), write out the six groups of letters that appear under each letter of the pattern. Place them in the alphabetical sequence of the letters along the top A first, D, E, G, N, and R.

A

ciex

D

ismx

E

rdax

G

ntsx

N

ahsx

R

eage

Here is your encoded message, which you can send. Your friend will receive the scrambled message and, using the agreed route and key word, will be able to decode it.

Here is the same message written out in groups of four letters. Can you tell which grid it was drawn on ?

sgxe
eexa
saxr
mxxd
lcan
siht

Answer
It is drawn on the SHADOW grid.

39

JUMBLED WORDS

1 EGASSEMSIHTDAE

2 EGAS·SEMS·IHTD·

3 SAGE·SMES·DTHI·

4 IARA·TIMS·AECN·

5 CINA·ERDA·HTSI·

6 IGASREASTHIDM

Six additional ways of arranging the letters of your message simply

RNACI

AERN·ACI

NREA·ICA

EDHS·ESG

EMSS·GAE

ESNA E

1 Write it backward.

2 Break the backward row into groups.

3 Reverse each group.

4 Write every second letter leaving out those between; then continue using the omitted letters.

5 Write out pairs of letters and reverse them; then join them to the next two.

6 Write every second letter with a gap between them; then work back through, placing the missing letters in gaps.

Leonardo da Vinci
(1452–1519)

The artist and scientist Leonardo made thousands of drawings and observations in his notebooks, recording details of shape and form and his ideas for inventions, but his notes appear to be written in a secret code. Leonardo was left-handed and his writing also goes from right to left. Hold it up in front of a mirror and you will be able to read it in the reflection – if your Italian is good enough!

Leonardo da Vinci

This is an enlarged sample of Leonardo's backward writing. On the facing page is how it would look if written from left to right. Below are the Italian letters written more clearly, and an English translation.

fa la forma di fori
di gesso per fuggire

fa la forma difori
di gesso per
fuggire

*... draw the figure on the
outside in chalk to flee ...*

45

MIRROR MAGIC

ищжэоль
ьэич цэгs
coир ioir

You can use Leonardo's method of writing
backward by simply writing onto tracing
paper with a thick pen and then turning it
over and pasting your message upside
down onto a white sheet. The reader must
then hold it against a mirror to be able to
read what you have written.

can you read this message

1 First write on tracing paper.

uoɔɔɘɓɔɒ *ɿɒ* *ʇɓ* *ɿɒɔ* *ʌɒ*

2 Turn the tracing paper over and paste it onto a sheet of ordinary paper.

can you read this message

3 The receiver holds a mirror up against your message to read it.

2 SUBSTITUTION CIPHERS

31·11·43: **55·53·15:**

54·32·42·44:

Substitution ciphers have been around for thousands of years – probably for as long as writing itself.

Substitution ciphers come in many forms but are essentially simple to create. A

34·51·11·41:

31·53·41·51:

See pages 56–57 to work it out!

message encoded using a substitution cipher has each of its letters switched to other letters, or perhaps things. For example, each letter could become a picture or a musical tone – in fact anything that works.

BASIC
SUBSTITUTION
CODE
V·PNA·ERNQ

The most basic substitution code is very
easy and quick to do.

A Write out the first thirteen letters of the
alphabet and underneath write out the
remaining thirteen.

B Write your message by replacing the

A BCDEFG
N OPQRST

GUVF·ZRFFNTR

letters in your message with those above or below yours. So *A* becomes *N*, and *T* becomes *G*. Alternatively you could substitute the first thirteen further by writing the lower row backward, so *A* becomes *Z*, *B* becomes *Y*, and so on.

HIJKLM
UVWXYZ

SHIFT CIPHERS

Shift ciphers have been around for thousands of years. Julius Caesar, the Roman dictator, had one named after him because he would use it when sending

KYZJ DVJJRXV

important messages
to his generals.

Romans in battle

Julius Caesar

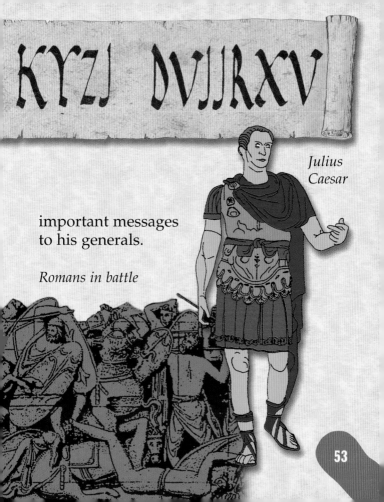

A	B	C	D	E	F	G	H	I	J	K	L	M

R	S	T	U	V	W	X	Y	Z	A	B	C	D

HOW TO ENCODE USING A SHIFT CIPHER

Write the alphabet in a row and choose a number to be your key number. In the example above the number is 10. Start from *A* and count along to the right your key number (in this case *J*) and write *A* directly below it. Continue to the right with *B*, *C* … until you reach *Z*, then go back to the beginning and finish your alphabet. A 10-shift cipher will look like the example above. For your friends to be able to decode your message, you will have to tell them your key number.

To encode a message find the letter in the top row and substitute it with the letter directly below it, in this example *I = Z*.

To decode a message find the letter in the bottom row and substitute it with the letter directly above it, in this example *Z = I*.

POLYBIUS CIPHER

Two thousand two hundred years ago a Greek called Polybius invented a very simple substitution code. Each letter of the alphabet was placed in a grid of five squares by five squares.

The squares were marked by numbers along the top – the columns – and numbers down the side – the rows. For example, letter *I*, being in the fourth column and the second row, is 42.

Today, X and Z may be placed in the same box since these are not often used in English.

42·44:33·51·44·44·11·22·51

	1	2	3	4	5
1	A	B	C	D	E
2	F	G	H	I	J
3	K	L	M	N	O
4	P	Q	R	S	T
5	U	V	W	X Z	Y

Polybius
(204–122 BC)

Polybius lived at a time when the Romans
were expanding their empire into North
Africa and the eastern Mediterranean,
which had been part of Greek civilization
until then. He witnessed the destruction of
the ancient city of Carthage by the
Romans and was appointed by them to
organize the government of the conquered
Greek cities.

Polybius the governor of Greek cities

The ancient city of Carthage before its destruction

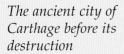

I knock knock-knock knock knock knock
C knock-knock knock knock
A knock-knock
N knock knock knock-knock knock knock knock
R knock knock knock knock-knock knock knock
E knock-knock knock knock knock kncok
A knock-knock
D knock-knock knock knock knock
T knock knock knock knock-knock knock knock knock knock
H knock knock-knock knock
I knock knock-knock knock knock knock
S knock knock knock knock-knock knock knock knock
M knock knock knock-knock knock knock
E knock-knock knock knock knock knock
S knock knock knock knock-knock knock knock knock
S knock knock knock knock-knock knock knock knock
A knock-knock
G knock knock-knock knock
E knock-knock knock knock knock knock

KNOCK KNOCK CIPHER

Prisoners used the Polybius grid to convey messages. Each square is represented by the number of knocks identifying the columns and rows.

number of knocks to locate the columns

→

number of knocks to locate the row

↓

	1	2	3	4	5
1	A	B	C	D	E
2	F	G	H	I	J
3	K	L	M	N	O
4	P	Q	R	S	T
5	U	V	W	X/Z	Y

LINEAR B

In 1900 the archeologist Sir Arthur Evans (1851–1941) discovered a large number of clay tablets at Knossos on Crete. He realized that the inscriptions on the tablets represented three different scripts: a "hieroglyphic" script, Linear A, and Linear B. Although archeologists have not been able to decipher the first two scripts so far, Linear B was solved by Michael Ventris (1922–56) in 1953 as representing the sounds of ancient Greek.

You and your friends can also substitute symbols for the sounds of English, creating your own secret language!

a	da	ja	ka	ma	na	pa
e	de	je	ke	me	ne	pe
i	di		ki	mi	ni	pi
o	do	jo	ko	ma	no	po
u	du	ju	ku	mu	nu	pu

qa	ra	sa	ta	wa	za
qe	re	se	te	we	ze
qi	ri	si	ti	wi	
qo	ro	so	to	wo	zo
ru	su	tu			

The Linear B sound symbols

Alberti
(1404–72)

Leone Battista Alberti
was educated in law
at the University of
Bologna, Italy.
After an illness
that caused him to
lose part of his
memory, he
abandoned his
career as a lawyer
and turned his
attention to science
and art instead.

Alberti was an
accomplished cryptographer – a writer of
secret messages – who invented many
ciphers that were *polyalphabetic* (use at
least two alphabets), and was an

early inventor of machine-aided encryption – his cipher disk. The **polyalphabetic cipher** was the most significant technical advance in cryptography since the time of Julius Caesar.

Alberti's 20-letter disks

The outer ring includes numbers 1 to 4 to make up 24 segments.

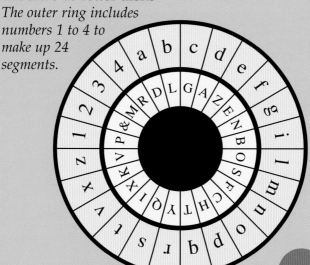

vpivnfyvwrh

THE ALBERTI DISK

The Alberti disk is a device consisting of two circular disks, each with the alphabet on the rim. You can make a set of disks just as Alberti did. By setting any letter on the minor disk against any other letter on the outer disk you are able to replace the letters of your message with coded letters. There are 32 spaces for 26 letters of the alphabet, so six letters can be duplicated by the addition of a six-letter word – in this case "donkey."

peoyeevky

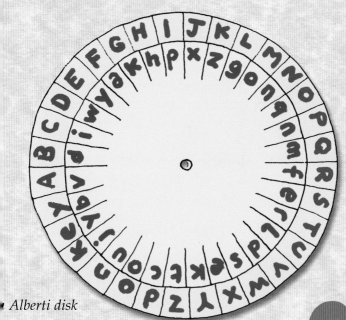

Alberti disk

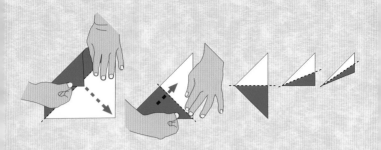

You can start making your two disks by folding a large square sheet of white paper over and over.

Fold one corner of each new triangle toward the other. Continue folding for a total of five times.

When finished you have a square sheet with folds divided into thirty-two sections.

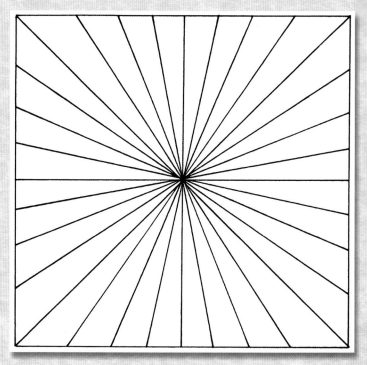

A square with 32 divisions around its center

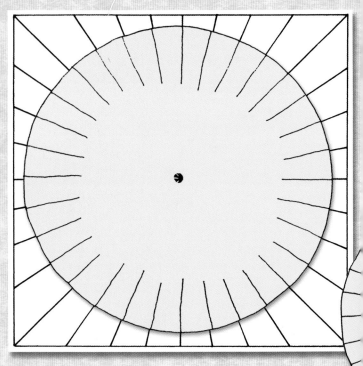

Add capital letters to this. Write the entire alphabet, then add a word of your choice.

Select two different colored pieces of cardboard and cut out circles. Now place the two cut-out circles (one smaller than the other) onto the squared grid. Mark off the 32 divisions on each.

Add lowercase letters to this in random order, including your chosen word.

ABAAA • AAABA • AAAAA • ABBAA
BAABA • AABBB • ABAAA • BAAAB
AAAAA • AABBA • AABAA

SEMAGRAMS

The word "semagram" is based upon the Greek *sema* which means "sign" and *gramma* which means "written" or "drawn": it describes a method of hiding a message.

Sir Francis Bacon, Lord Chancellor to Queen Elizabeth I of England (reigned 1558–1603), was one of the first people to propose such a system of coding messages.

Bacon created a clever form of stenography (shorthand), though it may not seem short to most people. The code used 24 letters with both *U* and *V*, and *I* and *J* interchangeable. Opposite is an alphabet Bacon created using the first two letters of his name.

BAAAA • AABAA • AAAAA • AAABB •
ABABB • AABAA • BAAAB • BAAAB •

*Sir Francis
Bacon
(1561–1626)*

a AAAAA	i ABAAA	r BAAAA
b AAAAB	k ABAAB	s BAAAB
c AAABA	l ABABA	t BAABA
d AAABB	m ABABB	v BAABB
e AABAA	n ABBAA	w BABAA
f AABAB	o ABBAB	x BABAB
g AABBA	p ABBBA	y BABBA
h AABBB	q ABBBB	z BABBB

59, 53, 51, 64, 68, 55, 54, 70, 58

Johannes Trithemius
(1462–1516)

Trithemius, a German abbot and counselor to Emperor Maximilian I, published three books about *steganography* (Greek for "hidden writing") and cryptography. The third of these books was considered by many people at the time to be a book about demons and monsters and was banned by the Catholic church. In fact it was a textbook about how to encrypt messages, which used the same principles as those underlying the World War II Enigma machine and modern cell phones. It seems that Trithemius's methods of

59,69,63,55,69,69,51,57,55.

steganography worked very well, as his ideas about encrypting messages remained hidden from view for nearly 500 years.

A	B	C	D	E	F	G	H	I	J	K	L	M
1	2	3	4	5	6	7	8	9	10	11	12	13

	I	C	A	N	R	E	A	D	T	H	I
	9	3	1	14	18	5	1	4	20	8	9
+25	34	28	26	39	43	30	26	29	45	33	34
+50	59	53	51	64	68	55	51	54	70	58	59

Trithemius's method of encrypting a
message was simply to substitute numbers
for letters, and every time a word
appeared in the message following its
initial appearance, the number of letters
in the alphabet he was using – 25 – was
added to each number that made up
the word.

As you can see from the example above
the first time the phrase appears in the

N	O	P	Q	R	S	T	U	V	W	X	Y	Z
14	15	16	17	18	19	20	21	22	23	24	25	26

S	M	E	S	S	A	G	E
19	13	5	19	19	1	7	5
44	38	30	44	44	26	32	30
69	63	55	69	69	51	57	55

message it would be encrypted as 9, 3, 1, 14, 18, 5, 1, 4, 20, 8, 9, 19, 13, 5, 19, 1, 7, 5. The second time it would appear as 34, 28, 26, 39, 43, 30, 26, 29, 45, 33, 34, 44, 38, 30, 44, 44, 26, 32, 30, and so on. The effect of this is that any word or phrase never appears the same twice. This simple technique made the job of the code-breaker much more difficult indeed.

Did you notice on page 76 the title code has the seventh number missing?
The missing number is 51.

ZODIAC CIPHER

The early practitioners of chemistry – called alchemists – used symbols and signs to encode their writings so that other alchemists could not learn their secrets. In medieval times, these alchemists sought to change metals such as lead or iron into precious metals such as gold or silver.

The most common set of symbols they used were those already used to represent the planets and the constellations. These symbols were originally used by astrologers who read fortunes by consulting the postitions of the planets in the heavens. The main symbols are those of the twelve houses of the zodiac. Other symbols represented the planets, the

Sun, the Moon, and the Earth. Alchemists replaced the letters of the alphabet with zodiac signs and other astrological symbols.

The signs of the
zodiac

A zodiac alphabet

| A | B | C | D | E | F | G |

| H | I | J | K | L | M |

| N | O | P | Q | R | S |

| T | U | V | W | X | Y | Z |

Did you notice on pages 80 and 81 the message was upside down and back to front? Turn the book around to read the message correctly.

Mary
Queen of Scots
(1542–87)

Mary Queen of Scots was the victim of a series of intrigues that involved cipher messages. She was a rival of Elizabeth I for the English throne in the 16th century. Feeling that her life was in danger, she used concealed writing to prevent her letters being read by her enemies.

Her messages were enciphered using a **nomenclator**, a system that consists of a codelike list of words and names, and a separate cipher alphabet.

85

b9wmHɔ
A B C   D E F

faɑʊoᴀk
G H I J K L

ʊoxⱷ:ᴙ
M N O P Q R

btɪᴛⱶ
S T U V W

moƗ
X Y Z

The facing page is the alphabet used by
Mary Queen of Scots, in which each letter
could be drawn by a shape that was
private to her and the person she wrote
it to.

*Copy this grid and draw the simple shapes you will
use in your message into each square.*

A	B	C	D	E	F
G	H	I	J	K	L
M	N	O	P	Q	R
S	T	U	V	W	X
Y	Z				

NOMENCLATORS

A nomenclator code is where a word from a secret list replaces words in the message. The states of the USA are used here, each of which has been designated a group of words that could be used in a message. So to tell your friend you received and understood his message you could reply:

ARIZONA.
NORTH DAKOTA.
IOWA.

This means "ME READ MESSAGE"

State	Code	State	Code
Alabama	enemy	Missouri	climb
Alaska	you	Montana	tunnel
Arizona	me	Nebraska	hide
Arkansas	money	Nevada	locked
California	escape	New Hampshire	repeat
Colorado	spy	New Jersey	dog
Connecticut	play	New Mexico	bike
Delaware	friend	New York	skate
District of		North Carolina	run
Columbia	code	North Dakota	read
Florida	captured	Ohio	ball
Georgia	come	Oklahoma	catch
Hawaii	go	Oregon	fast
Idaho	help	Pennsylvania	missed
Illinois	watch	Rhode Island	home
Indiana	you are	South Carolina	jump
	watched	South Dakota	catch
Iowa	message	Tennessee	find
Kansas	treasure	Texas	see
Kentucky	chase	Utah	under
Louisiana	inside	Vermont	over
Maine	outside	Virginia	open
Maryland	under	Washington	close
Massachusetts	fire	West Virginia	question
Michigan	above	Wisconsin	answer
Minnesota	below	Wyoming	end
Mississippi	together		

SPY PIE CODE

You can make an alphabet to use in your secret messages with any form or shape in which the letters of the aphabet are located on the basic design.

Little pie shapes are used in the quarter circle cipher. Dots figure as a substitution for letters. Each letter of the alphabet is represented by a quarter circle and a dot in one of seven possible positions, three around the outside and three on the inside with one at the corner of the shape.

It is important that the person you send your message to has numbered his parts of the circle in the same order.

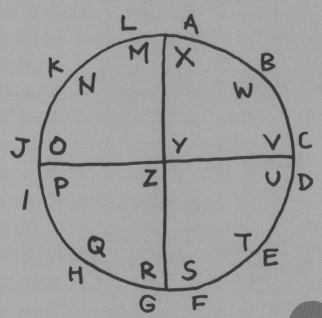

91

THE TRIPLE SQUARE CODE

This code is based upon the placing of three squares one within another.

Triangles are created by the overlapping squares, and a letter is then written in each triangle's corner. The key has to be drawn large enough for all the letters to fit.

If you decide to send a secret message using this cipher, you can draw all the triangles the same size.

The direction a triangle faces and the placement of the shaded corner inside will tell your friend what letter he needs to read from your secret message.

SKY HIGH CIPHER

If you look at the symbols opposite you will see that the whole alphabet fits in its nine different spaces or "rooms," with a question mark added after the letter Z.

You are able to represent each letter by a picture of the room it is in and by marking with a dot to indicate whether the letter is at the top, middle, or bottom of its room.

To further confuse those who might try to break your code, you can write out the message in columns. In the message on the left a letter has been left out: which one is it?

CALENDAR CODES

To use this code, you and your friends both need a grid calendar for the same year laid out in the same way. Your message is turned into code by substituting numbers for letters of the alphabet, then replacing them with the days of the week on the calendar month you have agreed upon.

December							week
Sun	Mon	Tue	Wed	Thu	Fri	Sat	
				1	**2**	**3**	1
4	**5**	**6**	**7**	**8**	**9**	**10**	2
11	**12**	**13**	**14**	**15**	**16**	**17**	3
18	**19**	**20**	**21**	**22**	**23**	**24**	4
25	**26**	**27**	**28**	**29**	**30**	**31**	5
Sun	Mon	Tue	Wed	Thu	Fri	Sat	

T3•M2•M4•M4•T#1•W2•M2

A	B	C	D	E	F	G	H	I	J	K	L	M
1	2	3	4	5	6	7	8	9	10	11	12	13

N	O	P	Q	R	S	T	U	V	W	X	Y	Z
14	15	16	17	18	19	20	21	22	23	24	25	26

- Write out the alphabet and below it a number for each letter.
- Write out your message and below it the numbers of the alphabet.

I CAN READ THIS MESSAGE
9–3•1•14–18•5•1•4–20•8•9•19–13•5•19•19•1•7•5

- Select a month of the year – in this case, December.
- The first message number is "9."
- Find the 9th day (Friday), and write down the initial *F* for Friday.

December							week
Sun	Mon	Tue	Wed	Thu	Fri	Sat	
				1	2	3	1
4	5	6	7	8	9	10	2
11	12	13	14	15	16	17	3
18	19	20	21	22	23	24	4
25	26	27	28	29	30	31	5
Sun	Mon	Tue	Wed	Thu	Fri	Sat	

December							week
Sun	Mon	Tue	Wed	Thu	Fri	Sat	
				1	2	3	1
4	5	6	7	8	9	10	2
11	12	13	14	15	16	17	3
18	19	20	21	22	23	24	4
25	26	27	28	29	30	31	5
Sun	Mon	Tue	Wed	Thu	Fri	Sat	

- Select which week has the 9th day (in this case it's the 2nd week).
- So the first code letter *I* is number 9, which is *F2* in this month. Your second letter to be coded, *C*, is number 3 which is *S* (for Saturday) and *1* (for the first week) – *S1*.

- If the number falls on a Thursday or Sunday mark these as T# or S# to distinguish them from Tuesday and Saturday.

"Ko-Ki, Bi

PHONE CIPHER

You can easily use a grid code with a group of friends where each letter of the alphabet has its own distinctive sound. With these conversations you can talk to your friend over the phone in coded words. Both of you must have the same color grid.

Make sure your friend has the grid by the side of his phone to enable him to convert the sounds you make back to the letters on the blue grid.

You will have noticed the top and bottom green rows are vowels. When you say one of the letters in the yellow columns combined with a vowel, you get thirty different sounds.

Du- Nu, Zi, Bi, Gi-...→

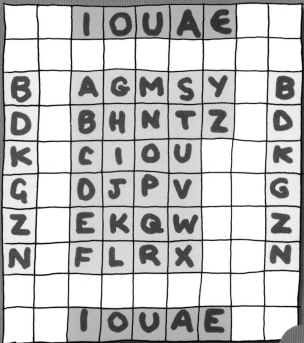

101

Da, Do, Ko, Ba,— Bu, Z

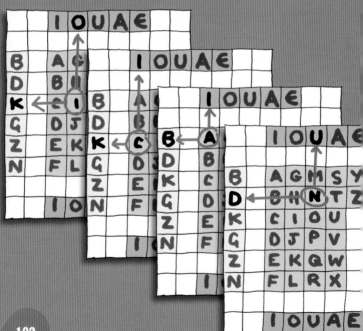

Ba, Ba, Bi, Bo, Zi"

How to say your code

- Write out your plaintext message with a space between each letter.
- Begin with the first letter of your message and place your finger on it on the blue area.
- Move your finger along the grid to the yellow box on the side (this is *K*).
- Move your finger to a green box above or below your first letter (this is *O*).
- Now write down the combination of the two (KO). This represents the first letter of your coded message.
- Continue by selecting a yellow and green letter for each of the letters of your message.
- You can now read out each word in the coded groups, leaving a pause between each pronunciation.

B
D
K
G
Z
N

SING ME A MESSAGE

Edward Elgar, the famous English composer, was fascinated by all forms of puzzles. He himself has left us the *Dorabella* cipher. On July 14, 1897, Elgar sent a letter to a young friend, the 22 year-old Miss Dora Penny. An odd feature of the letter was that it was in a cipher which still presents a challenge to us. An equal challenge is Elgar's *Enigma*

Variations, his most popular work. The work remains tantalizing to "musical detectives" for the hidden "messages" the composer wove into the score.

But can you make music that carries a secret message for a friend? Choose an opera or a popular song. Your friend should substitute the numbers he receives for letters in the libretto/lyrics so that he can read the message you have sent him. It will be easy for him to decipher your message. Far easier than finding the libretto, you might say.

John Wilkins
(1614–72)

In England during the 1650s there was a disastrous civil war. Families, friends, workers, and landowners fought over whether the country should be ruled by the King or Parliament. Those who supported King Charles were royalists, while those who supported his opponent Oliver Cromwell were parliamentarians.

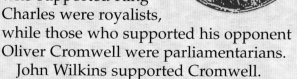

John Wilkins supported Cromwell. Although a churchman, Wilkins was a keen supporter of science and all ideas that had a rational basis. He was a major supporter of those interested in science and helped found the British Royal Society of Science.

During his involvement in the English Civil War he wrote a short book, *Mercury, or The Secret and Swift Messenger* in which he explained how secret codes could help convey messages between friends.

MUSICAL CODE

Mercury, or The Secret and Swift Messenger was published during Cromwell's rebellion in England (1641–66) as a warning to those who betrayed war plans by using poor cipher systems.

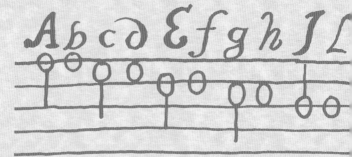

"Where the five vowels are represented by the minnums on each of the five lines being most of them placed according to their right Order and Consequence only the letters K and Q are left out because they may be otherwise expressed … By this you may easily discern how two Musicians may discourse with one another by playing upon their Instruments of Musick as well as by talking with their Instruments of Speech."

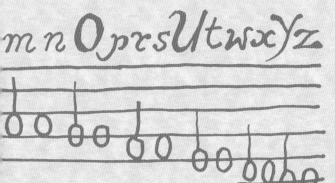

WILKINS'S STRING CIPHER

One of the ciphers Wilkins mentions in his *Mercury, or The Secret and Swift Messenger* is the *string cipher*. To use the string cipher you will need a piece of cardboard, and whoever you are sending the message to will need an identical card, with the alphabet along the top and a series of notches cut down each side. A length of string is knotted at one end, and the knot is put into the first notch. The string is then taken across the card, looped around the notch on the opposite side and then back across the card, and so on until all the notches are used. You then make marks on the string to indicate the letters in your message. The string is then removed from the card and sent to

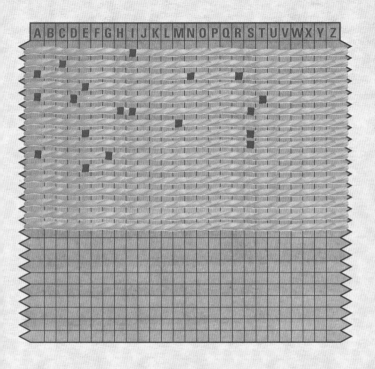

| A | B | C | D | E | F | G | H | I | J | K | L | M | N | O | P | Q | R | S | T | U | V | W | X | Y | Z |

your friends. Can you read the message on the string above?

MORSE CODE

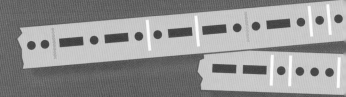

▼ Morse code is a letter substitution system.

▼ Each letter is replaced by a combination of dots and dashes.

▼ This was devised to permit the transmission of an electrical impulse of a short or long time interval.

▼ The elements of a dot can be obtained by momentary contact with a transmitter and a dash by longer contact.

▼ The combinations and intervals are all transmitted as common time units:

    a) A dash is the length of three dots.

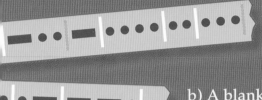

b) A blank interval between the dot and dash components of each group represents a letter equal to one dot.

c) The interval between words by a space is equal to five dots.

▼ The original group of combinations for both letters and numerals was devised so that the most frequent letters are given brief groups, for example *E* has only one dot, and *T* has only one dash.

▼ Less common letters have a larger number of elements.

▼ *J* has a dot and three dashes.

MORSE CODE ALPHABET

●▬   ▬●●●   ▬●▬●   ▬●●
A   **B**   **C**   **D**

●   ●●▬●   ▬▬●   ●●●●
E   **F**   **G**   **H**

●●   ●▬▬▬   ▬●▬   ●▬●●
I   **J**   **K**   **L**

▬▬   ▬●   ▬▬▬   ●▬▬●
M   **N**   **O**   **P**

▬▬●▬   ●▬●   ●●●   ▬
Q   **R**   **S**   **T**

●●▬   ●●●▬   ●▬▬   ▬●●▬
U   **V**   **W**   **X**

Y **Z** **1** **2**

3 **4** **5** **6**

7 **8** **9** **0**

period comma question mark colon

semicolon quotation marks apostrophe hyphen

understand wait error end of message

Samuel Morse
(1791–1872)

The Morse code was devised so that the
letters of the alphabet could be sent on
an electric current through a wire to a
distant receiver. It was invented by
American Samuel Morse in 1837.
Morse, who was an artist, entered an
American government competition to
devise a method of transmitting
messages across the Atlantic. In 1843 he
won the prize of $30,000, and within ten
years, America had 50 telegraph
companies erecting continuous line
connections across the United States,
South America, and Europe.

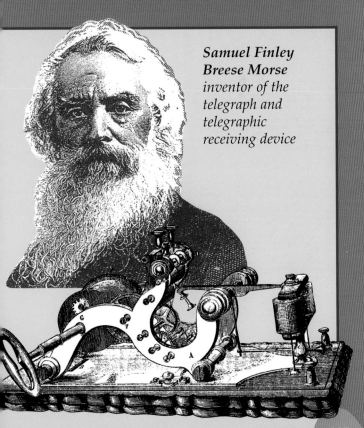

Samuel Finley Breese Morse
inventor of the telegraph and telegraphic receiving device

DANCING MEN

▼ This is a substitution cipher.

▼ There are many methods of writing out cipher alphabets where each letter is replaced by a symbol, figure, letter, or number.

▼ The simplest is to draw rows of dancing men where each letter is represented by a different gesture. You choose what they are doing.

▼ First write each letter into a box on grid paper, then above it add a simple drawing in which the positions of the arms and legs are different.

▼ Next write your message using dancing men instead of letters.

▼ At the end of each word have the stick man hold a flag or balloon.

▼ Your friend needs a copy of your 26 dancing men.

▼ Turn over to the next page to see our range of figures.

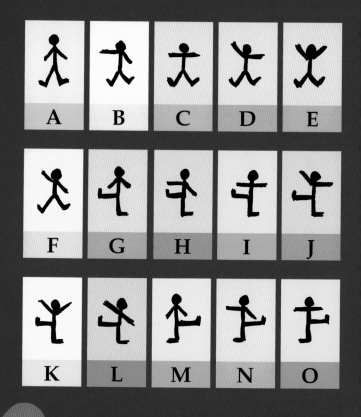

A B C D E

F G H I J

K L M N O

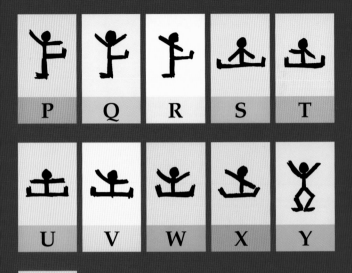

P Q R S T

U V W X Y

Z

SHERLOCK HOLMES, SUPER DETECTIVE

"Why, Holmes, it's a child's drawing," cried Dr Watson when he first saw the figures opposite penciled on a page torn from a notebook. But Sherlock Holmes recognized it immediately as a substitution cipher. The message was: AM HERE ABE SLANEY. The little flags marked the ends of words.

"I am fairly familiar with all forms of secret writing," Holmes declared, "and am myself the author of a trifling monograph upon the subject, in which I analyze one hundred and sixty separate ciphers …"

Sherlock Holmes solved this Dancing Men cipher message

Arthur Conan Doyle, creator of Sherlock Holmes

ADAPTING A SUDOKU GRID

Open any of the daily papers in America and you'll see a sudoku puzzle, also known as a Number Place.

The aim of the puzzle is to enter a number from 1 through 9 in each cell of a 9 x 9 grid made up of 3 x 3 subgrids (called "regions"), starting with various numerals given in some cells (the "givens"). Each row, column, and region must contain only one instance of each numeral.

62|26|27|61 · 43|17|61|61|7|25|17

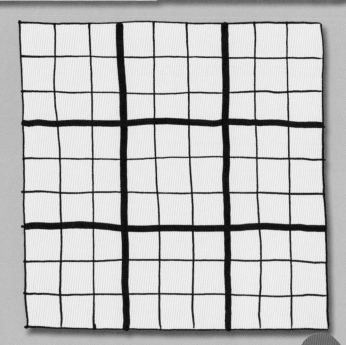

A sudoku grid

1	2	3	4	5	6	7	8	9
10	11	12	13	14	15	16	17	18
19	20	21	22	23	24	25	26	27
28	29	30	31	32	33	34	35	36
37	38	39	40	41	42	43	44	45
46	47	48	49	50	51	52	53	54
55	56	57	58	59	60	61	62	63
64	65	66	67	68	69	70	71	72
73	74	75	76	77	78	79	80	81

All you and your friend have to agree upon is the position of the English alphabet in the sudoku grid (9 x 9). All cells should be marked by numbers and 26 cells should also contain letters.

A message made up of numbers is then sent to your friend. He or she will have to substitute the numbers with letters to be able to read it.

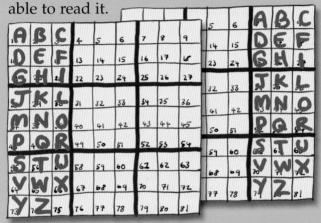

Here only the last column of squares has been used. You could use this and then the first columns on the next occasion. Then tell your friend which by beginning the message with *L* or *R*. You could use the top rows or bottom and mark *T* or *B* before the message.

CHESS

Chess has been played for more than 700 years. This means that people have had a chance to send secret messages using chess notation for all this time.

For those who are still unfamiliar with it, the chessboard is a square divided into 8 columns and 8 rows (a total of 64 squares). When recording the moves in a chess game the squares in the horizontal rows are marked by a number from *1* to *8* and the columns are marked by lower case letters of the alphabet *a* to *h*.

c1a1f3　b5e1a1d1

d5h1a3c5

a8	b8	c8	d8	e8	f8	g8	h8
a7	b7	c7	d7	e7	f7	g7	h7
a6	b6	c6	d6	e6	f6	g6	h6
a5	b5	c5	d5	e5	f5	g5	h5
a4	b4	c4	d4	e4	f4	g4	h4
a3	b3	c3	d3	e3	f3	g3	h3
a2	b2	c2	d2	e2	f2	g2	h2
a1	b1	c1	d1	e1	f1	g1	h1

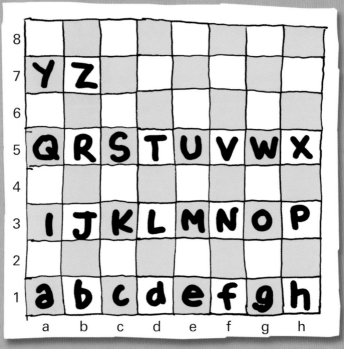

You can place the alphabet in any rows upward or across, but your friend must have the same placements.

To send a secret message you don't even have to know how to play. But it is essential you agree with your friends where the letters of the English alphabet will be placed on the board. If you place them in every second row starting with *a1* for the letter *a*, the message "I can read this message" will read

**a3 c1a1f3 b5e1a1d1
d5h1a3c5
e3e1c5c5a1g1e1**

BOXING A POEM

Make a grid of 100 squares or photocopy a graph paper grid of squares.

Your grid will have ten squares along the top and ten down the side. Number the rows along the edge.

Select a poem you and your friend know, for example *The Star Spangled Banner*:

*Oh, say can you see by the dawn's early light
What so proudly we hailed at the
twilight's last gleaming?
Whose broad stripes and bright stars
through the perilous fight
O'er the ramparts we watched
were so gallantly streaming?
And the rockets' red glare,
the bombs bursting in air,
Gave proof through the night
that our flag was still there.*

73.82.88.96.79.49.66.84.59.

	1	2	3	4	5	6	7	8	9	10
1										
2										
3										
4										
5										
6										
7										
8										
9										
10										

	1	2	3	4	5	6	7	8	9	10
1	o	h	s	a	y	c	a	n	y	o
2	u	s	e	e	b	y	t	h	e	d
3	a	w	n	s	e	a	r	l	y	l
4	i	g	h	t	w	h	a	t	s	o
5	p	r	o	u	d	l	y	w	e	h
6	a	i	l	e	d	a	t	t	h	e
7	t	w	i	l	i	g	h	t	s	l
8	a	s	t	g	l	e	a	m	i	n
9	g	w	h	o	s	e	b	r	o	a
10	d	s	t	z	x	v	q	k	j	f

The selected text written into the squares with missing alphabet letters in the last line.

134

- First write out your selected lines of prose or poetry in the first nine rows, then cross out each letter of the alphabet in turn.
- If the alphabet letter is not used in the sentences then write that letter in row ten beginning at the last box and working backward along the row.
- You now have 100 spaces filled with words containing all the letters of the alphabet.
- These letters are not used in the first ninety letters of my poem – *zx vqkjf*.

The important feature of this code is that individual letters can have many code interpretations.
- The letter *I* can be 41, 62, 73, 75, and 89.
- The letter *e* can be 23, 24, 29, 35, 59, 64, 610, 86, 96. Whichever number you choose to represent a letter you can then change to another number to

This is the order of the numbers for the nineteen letters in your message:

41, 16, 14, 33, 37, 64, 47, 101, 44, 46, 73, 82, 88, 96, 79, 49, 66, 84, 59.

represent the same letter on the next occasion.

- Without knowing the original text selected by you and your friend, the code-breaker cannot fill in the squares on a grid with letters, and they cannot follow the frequency of letters occurring in your message as letters are represented by changing numbers.
- Another way of using a poem is simply

This is the same message but with a different selection of numbers:

75, 16, 81, 810, 98, 23, 47, 65, 78, 93, 89, 95, 88, 86, 95, 79, 910, 76, 29.

to tell your friend secretly which poem you are using. Then, later, send your secret message quoting the line and the position of the letters along the line.

- The first number in each group is the line and the second number is the letter selected along the line.

PLOTTING CIPHERS

It is possible to disguise a message as a picture. Or you may send it as an important looking graph.

The dot cipher message and one way to hide it

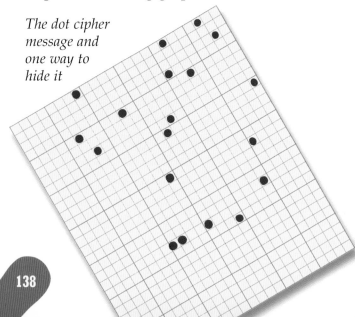

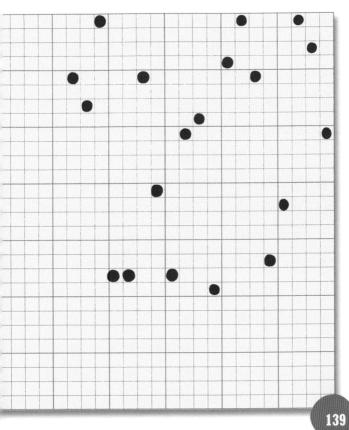

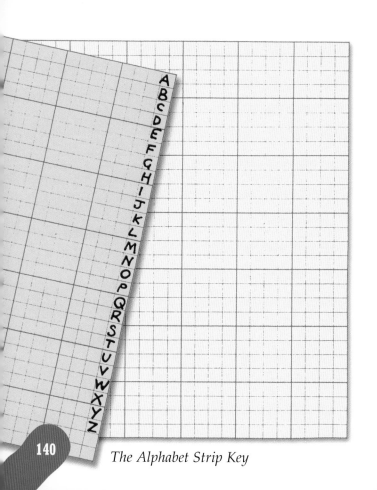

A B C D E F G H I J K L M N O P Q R S T U V W X Y Z

140

The Alphabet Strip Key

Firstly, you need to make an Alphabet Strip Key. On a strip of graph paper write the alphabet in a column. Make marks at the top and bottom. Your friend will need one just like it, and a pad of the same graph paper.

To decode a message with the Alphabet Strip Key, put the key along the right edge of a piece of graph paper. Mark arrows on the paper next to the ticks on the Key, with the same position for the rows of the grid. This will help your friend to decode your message later. Put a dot on the graph paper next to the first letter of your message on the last vertical line. Move backward to the next vertical line, and put a dot next to the second letter of your message. Continue working right to left, putting dots next to the letters of your message.

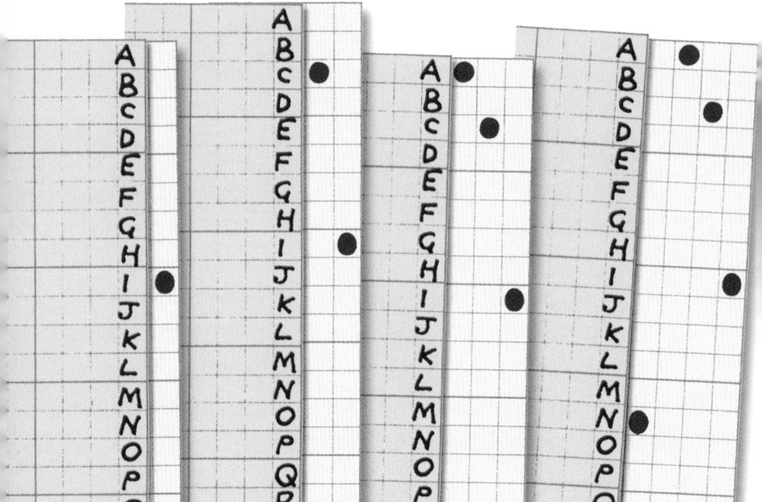
ABCDEFGHIJKLMNOPQRSTUVWXYZ
ABCDEFGHIJKLMNOPQRSTUVWXYZ
ABCDEFGHIJKLMNOPQRSTUVWXYZ
ABCDEFGHIJKLMNOPQRSTUVWXYZ
I C A N

When you have completed plotting your message you will have a piece of graph paper with dots placed where you located each letter in the message.

Since the message moves right to left, you can disguise it by connecting the dots to make a graph or even a crazy picture.

To decode the message, line up your Alphabet Strip Key with the ends of the markers. Slowly move the key from right to left, and read off the letters next to the dots.

Plotting the letters I, C, A, N (left)
Note the order of your secret message will be from right to left.

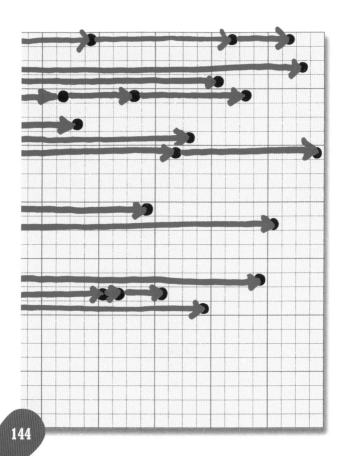

By joining the dots horizontally your message is further hidden as the decoder thinks each dot has some horizontal link – whereas you know they have a vertical sequence and are read from right to left.

The furthest extended dot is the first letter and its vertical position – nine squares down – means it's the ninth letter *I*. You can hide your letters in many ways that will confuse people who want to read your thoughts. This wiggly line has nothing to do with how the dots indicate the alphabet letters.

Two ways to hide the dot sequence

Blaise de Vigenère
(1523–96)

Blaise de Vigenère was a French diplomat in the 16th century. During the 30 years of his service for the Duke of Nevers, Europe was in a constant state of warfare over which way to follow Christianity. The wars were between and within countries, between Catholics and Protestants. Blaise worked for the Catholic authorities, and it was important to him that decisions and messages passed across Europe could not be read by the Protestants.

In one of his books *The Theory of Ciphers* (1585), he describes his invention, an autokey cipher. It was the first cipher to use a method where the same letters could be replaced by others at each encodement. The same message could be written in a variety of ways.

French Protestants tortured by Catholics

AUTOKEY CIPHER

	1.	2.	3.	4.	5.	6.	7.	8.	9.		12.	13.	14.	15.	16
L.	l.														
M.													y		
N.		n		n										n	
O.															
P.							.							n	
R.															
S.	s.	s													
T.															
V.		u		u	u										
A.			a										٠		
B.	.														
C.	c		c												
			c												
D.														G	o
E.	c	e.													
		e													
H.			h												
I.		i		i											

18.	19.	20.	
	—		I
			H
c			E
	d		D
			C
			B
2			A
c	c	c	V
		i	T
	n	v	S
			R
			P
c		o	O
n	n		N
m			M
5.	4.	2.	L

Vigenère had a book containing a grid of 100 squares. The downward columns were numbered and the rows across were letters of the alphabet. Inside each square he could place letters in five positions – the four corners and the center. He therefore had 500 locations for the letters of this message.

a   b

e

d   c

How Vigenère hid his message

Vigenère disguised his coded message by drawing a picture over the position of the letters. Here he uses stars (for the positions) and clouds to hide their relationships.

Here he uses a bush
with the position of
the letters marked
with berries.

Thomas Jefferson
(1743–1826)

As well as being president, Thomas Jefferson was an inventor. While serving as George Washington's Secretary of State (1790–93), he devised a secure method for encoding and decoding messages – the wheel cipher.

The device had 26 wooden disks threaded

Thomas Jefferson

onto a spindle. The alphabet was scrambled on each disk in a different order. To send a message to his friend,

Jefferson rotated each disk until the letters formed the message he wanted. His message did not contain any punctuation or spaces. Then he looked at any one of the other lines on the cipher wheel and wrote that line down, sending it as the encoded message.

His ally had a cipher wheel with the same order of letters and disks as Jefferson's. The ally lined up the letters from the encoded message and then looked around the wheel until he found a line that made sense.

George Washington

JEFFERSON'S CIPHER WHEEL

The message "I can read this message" can be enciphered if you turn the first wheel to the *I*, the second wheel to the *C*, the third wheel to the *A*, and so on. The appearance on the wheel cipher is then: *icanreadthismessage*.

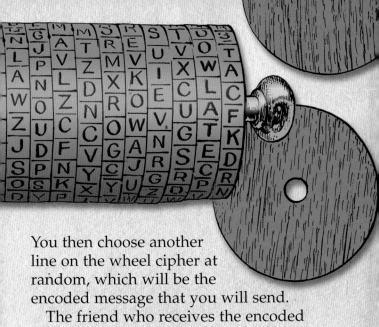

You then choose another line on the wheel cipher at random, which will be the encoded message that you will send.

The friend who receives the encoded message then turns the first wheel to the first letter of the cipher, the second wheel to its second letter, and so on. He or she then looks for a different line on the wheel that spells out a message that makes sense.

155

PIRATES' CODE

In the 18th century pirates of the Caribbean were a constant danger to the Spanish and British sailing ships crossing the Atlantic with goods taken from the newly discovered Americas.

"Black Heart Jack" and his second mate "One-Eyed Pete" were captured by British marines and were to be hanged for crimes on the ocean. One-Eyed Pete was the first to be questioned, and he sent a coded message to Jack.

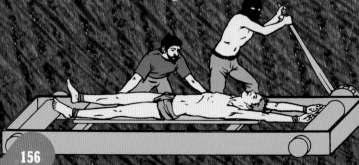

It read:

J upme uifn opuijoh

Pete was hanged – but Jack was unable to
read this simple message. When it was
Jack's turn to be questioned, he told them
everything about his crimes. Had he
untangled the message, it would have
read:

I told them nothing

This was a simple substitution code
where the secret message used the letter
after each one intended.

CITIZENS' BAND

Citizens' Band Radio (CB) is a short-distance voice communications service.

In 1934, the Federal Communications Commission (FCC) was established to supervise all radio and telecommunications. Three categories of radio services were created: Broadcast, Public, and Safety/Special.

A step forward was made by the development and installation of military radios in tanks during World War II. In 1944, Admiral Hooper suggested that a band of radio frequencies be set aside for returning veterans. He thought that the men could create a new "personal communications" industry.

In 1957, the FCC allocated the 27 megahertz frequencies to the Class D Citizens' Band Radio. In 1977, the number of available channels was increased to 40. Channel 9 was limited to emergency use only, and operators no longer needed a license to operate a CB radio.

During the early 1970s, oil shortages and labor strikes in the American trucking industry meant truck drivers needed to be able to communicate with the home base of the company they were working for. The CB radio became their primary means of communication.

As CB radio became a popular hobby, nontruckers set up stations in their garages, bedrooms, and basements. Although the introduction of cellular phones has decreased the number of CB operators, CB radios are still the main form of communication between truckers. CB radio operators identify themselves by using a "handle" – nickname.

10-1	Receiving poorly	10-16	Make pickup at
10-2	Receiving well	10-17	Urgent business
10-3	Stop transmitting	10-18	Anything for us?
10-4	OK, message received	10-19	Nothing for you, return to base
10-5	Relay message	10-20	My location is
10-6	Busy, stand by	10-21	Call by telephone
10-7	Out of service, leaving air	10-22	Report in person to
10-8	In service subject to call	10-23	Stand by
10-9	Repeat message	10-24	Completed last assignment
10-10	Transmission completed, standing by	10-25	Can you contact
10-11	Talking too rapidly	10-26	Disregard last information
10-12	Visitors present	10-27	I am moving to channel
10-13	Advise weather/road conditions	10-28	Identify your station
		10-29	Time is up for contact

The main CB radio numbers

10-41 Please turn to channel	**10-71** Proceed with transmission in sequence
10-42 Traffic accident at	
10-43 Traffic tie-up at	**10-77** Negative contact
10-44 I have a message for you	**10-81** Reserve hotel room for
10-45 All units within range please report	**10-82** Reserve room for
	10-84 My telephone number is
10-50 Break channel	**10-85** My address is
10-60 What is next message number?	**10-91** Talk closer to microphone
10-62 Unable to copy, use phone	**10-93** Check my frequency on this channel
10-63 Net decided to	
10-64 Net clear	**10-94** Please give me a long count
10-65 Awaiting your next message/assignment	
	10-99 Mission completed all units secure
10-67 All units comply	
10-70 Fire at	**10-200** Police needed at

Their transmissions are limited to five continuous minutes to make sure everyone has access. When your five minutes are up, you must remain silent for at least one minute before transmitting again. Since they are not allowed long conversations, the CB 10-codes were developed as a means of sending short messages.

3 SIGNS, SIGNALS, AND SYMBOLS

Sometimes you might wish that your parents or teachers used signs, signals, or symbols instead of preaching for hours. At other times you'd rather talk than stare at those incomprehensible mathematical symbols in your notebook. Signs,

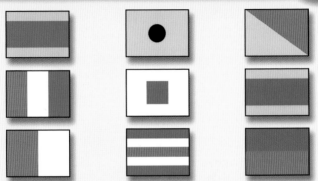

See pages 200–201 to work it out!

signals, and symbols are the fastest means of human communication and are priceless in times of danger or war. But both our everyday life and the history of art teaches us that we couldn't do without them even in peacetime.

TALK WITHOUT SOUND

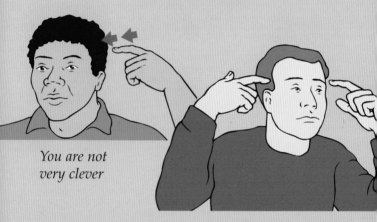

You are not very clever

You are stupid

You can use your face and hands to tell your friends what you think of others.

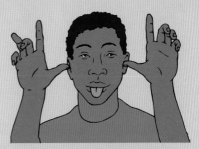

You are stupid,
so go away!

Go away!

Parents consider all of these gestures rude,
but they have been used by boys and girls
for generations.

I KNOW WHAT YOU ARE

The people of Naples seem to talk more with their hands than they do with their tongues. This is not just to add emphasis to what they are saying: for centuries Neapolitans have used gestures with very exact meanings. Here are some examples:

1 Be silent!
2 No
   3 Beauty
      4 Hunger
         5 Derision
            6 Tiredness
            7 Stupidity
            8 Beware
            9 Dishonest
            10 Crafty

TICK-TACK-TALK

2 to 1	3 to 1	4 to 1
hand over mouth	*hand under chin*	*hand flapping*

At the races, the men who take your money for betting on horses – bookmakers – send messages to their associates about what odds are being offered. The odds are the number of times your winnings are multiplied by your bet. Ten dollars on a favorite winner could win you a prize of twenty dollars at 2 to 1 – but ten dollars on a horse with a poor record with odds of 10 to 1 would win you $100 if it won the race.

5 to 1
hand on shoulder

6 to 1
from shoulder to
top of head

7 to 1
from shoulder
to face

8 to 1
from shoulder to
under chin

9 to 1
right hand flapping
left on top of head

10 to 1
hands clenched
on chest

ONE HAND COUNTING

If you are ever in a secret Chinese gambling den, you may want to convey your knowledge of the game's progress using ancient Chinese hand signals. One to five is easy, but 6 to 10 require you to learn special positions for your fingers.

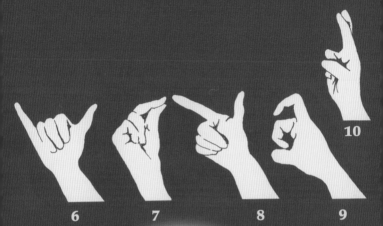

6 7 8 9 **10**

171

MUDRAS

Mudras are symbolic gestures made with the hand or fingers. In India, they are used in yoga meditation practice and Indian classical dance. Each mudra has a specific meaning, and they are a central part of Hindu iconography. With the arrival of

Buddhism, many mudra practices were absorbed into the culture. Common hand gestures are to be seen in both Hindu and Buddhist iconography. An example would be the outward-facing open palm known as Abhay (without fear) mudra, a gesture meant to dispel the fear of the devotee. In the classical dance of India different mudras represent animals, flowers, etc., as is shown on the next two pages.

An Indian dancer, a figure, mural, or sculpture can convey a secret meaning by the shape and positions of the hands.

Perching pigeon

Lotus in bloom

Flying pigeon

Deer

Budding lotus

To see

To speak

HAND TALK

Each of the different native peoples of the plains of central North America have their own languages. Pawnee, Shoshone, Arapaho, Cheyenne, Crow, and Sioux nations can talk and write amongst themselves but not between tribes.

When the Spanish first traded horses with the different tribes, the traders began to introduce a sign language, which enabled them to exchange news and goods with each other.

Anger

Exchange

Below

Lie

Council

177

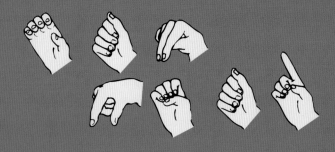

SIGN LANGUAGE

Visual means of communicating using gestures, facial expressions, and body language is called **sign language**. It is mainly used by deaf people or those with hearing difficulties.

American Sign Language (ASL) is the predominant sign language, particularly in the deaf communities in the United States, English-speaking Canada, and parts of Mexico. Although the United Kingdom and the United States share English as a spoken language, the prevalent form of sign language in Britain is called

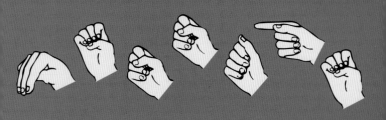

British Sign Language (BSL). As a language, it is neither dependent on nor strongly related to spoken English. BSL is the preferred language of 50,000–70,000 people in the United Kingdom.

ASL and BSL are not mutually intelligible.

The grammar and syntax of ASL are different from the spoken language. As for the number of people who use ASL as their primary language, estimates range from 500,000 to 2 million in the United States alone.

AMERICAN ALPHABET

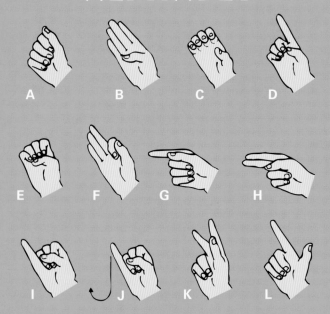

A　B　C　D

E　F　G　H

I　J　K　L

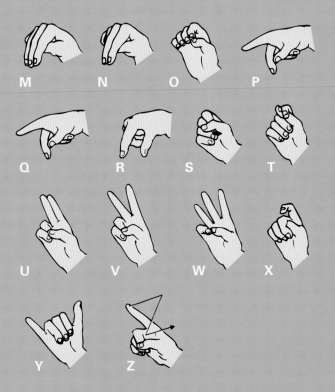

M   N   O   P

Q   R   S   T

U   V   W   X

Y   Z

Capitals are indicated by making a clockwise circle around each letter.

AMERICAN NUMBERS

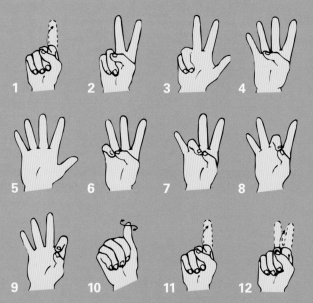

1 2 3 4

5 6 7 8

9 10 11 12

13

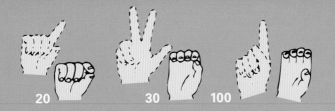

20   **30**   **100**

1,000

1 *The outstretched index finger of one hand.*

2 *Index and middle finger are outstretched; thumb, ring finger, and little finger are curled.*

3 *Thumb, index, and middle finger are outstretched; ring finger and little finger are curled.*

4 *Four fingers are stretched. Thumb is curled.*

5 *All fingers on one hand are outstretched.*

6 *Thumb and little finger are curled; index, middle, and ring finger are outsretched.*

7 *Thumb and ring finger are curled; index, middle, and little finger are outstretched.*

8 *Thumb and middle finger are curled; index, ring, and little finger are outstretched.*

9 *Thumb and index finger are curled; other fingers are outstretched.*

10 *All fingers but thumb are curled; thumb circles around.*

BRITISH ALPHABET

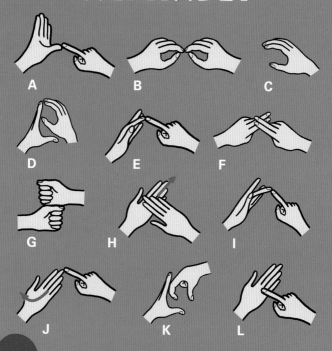

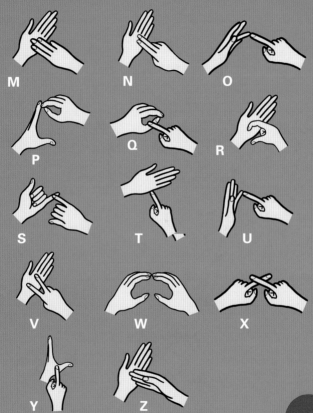

185

BRITISH NUMBERS

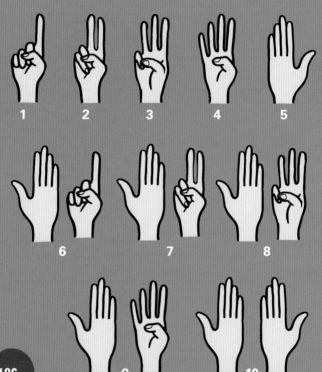

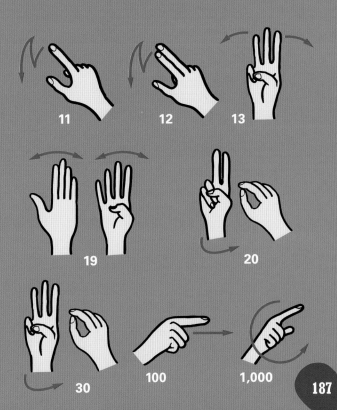

11

12

13

19

20

30

100

1,000

SEMAPHORE

Semaphore is sending messages by signals you make with your arms. You and a friend can learn to wave your arms about, making individual shapes to represent letters.

This method of sending messages was first used by the French during the revolutionary period of the 1790s.

The news required by armies confronting unseen enemies was relayed by soldiers waving flags from one hilltop to another.

Napoleon made great use of this method. For a hundred years this method was a valuable form of military communication.

INTERNATIONAL
SEMAPHORE POSITIONS

a & 1
b & 2
c & 3
d & 4
e & 5
f & 6
g & 7
h & 8
i & 9

j &
alphabetical
k & zero
l

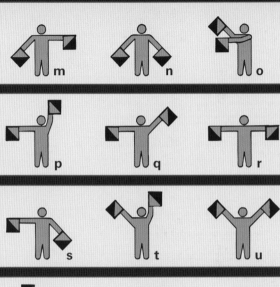

m

n

o

p

q

r

s

t

u

v

w

x

y

z

numeral

191

Claude Chappe
(1763–1805)

Claude Chappe was born in Brulon,
France. His early interest in science was
encouraged by his uncle, an astronomer
and traveler himself.

Chappe began developing his
semaphore system when he and his four
brothers lost their livelihoods in the
French Revolution.

The first Chappe semaphore line was
established between Paris and Lille in
1792. It was used to carry dispatches
during the war between France and
Austria. Other lines were then built,
including a line from Paris to Toulon.

193

The first symbol of a message to Lille would pass 120 miles (193 km) through 15 stations in only nine minutes. The speed of the line varied with the weather, but the line to Lille typically transferred 36 symbols, a complete message, in about 32 minutes.

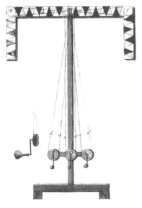

The hand-powered signal machine

By 1824, the Chappe brothers were promoting the semaphore lines for commercial use, especially to transmit the costs of commodities.

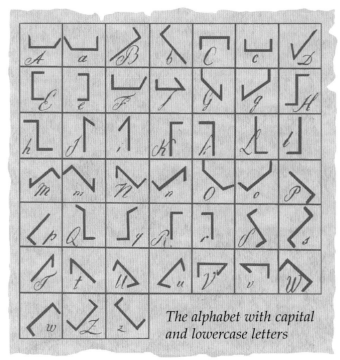

The alphabet with capital and lowercase letters

RACING

To assist racing drivers who are flashing past at 150 miles per hour, international organizations have a series of flags that can be waved to them to pass on information.

FLAGS

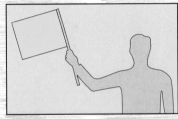

Yellow
A warning flag to indicate an obstruction, forbidding overtaking.

Red and yellow stripes

A warning flag to indicate oil or water on the track.

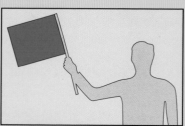

Green

Indicates the all clear.

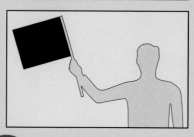

Black

A warning flag to indicate the race has been stopped. If it carries a driver's racing number, the driver must report to the pit lane.

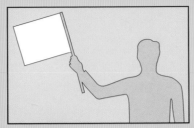

White
A warning flag to indicate that there is a service vehicle on the circuit.

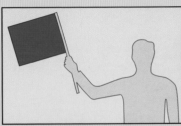

Blue
A warning flag to indicate that the driver is being followed closely by another competitor.

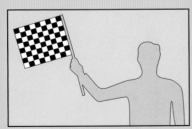

Checkered flag
The best-known flag signals the end of the race.

200

THE NAVAL FLAG CODE

Flags have long been used to identify ships' nationalities and to convey clear messages. Flags of different patterns and colors form an internationally recognized code for the letters of the alphabet and each also has a meaning of its own when flown individually.

The next pages show which flags are used to represent the alphabet and numbers. The alphabet flags have a double meaning (listed below the flags).

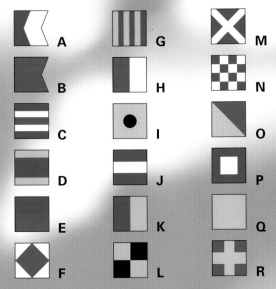

A *I am undergoing speed trials*

B *I have explosives on board*

C *Yes*

D *Keep clear, I am in difficulties*

E *I am altering course to starboard*

F *I am disabled*

G *I require a pilot*

H *Pilot is on board*

I *I am altering course to port*

J *I am sending a message by semaphore*

K *Stop at once*

L *Stop, I wish to communicate with you*

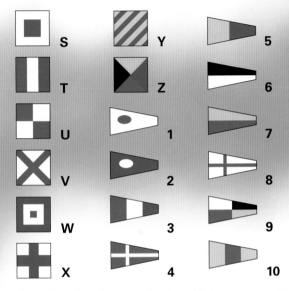

M *A doctor is on board*
N *No*
O *Man overboard*
P *(The Blue Peter): I am about to sail*
Q *Quarantine flag*
R *I have stopped*
S *I am going astern*
T *Do not pass ahead of me*
U *You are in danger*

V *I need help*
W *Send a doctor*
X *Stop, and watch for my signals*
Y *I am carrying mail*
Z *I am calling a shore station*

1–10 *Numbers*

CALLING FOR HELP

N & C flying together means *in distress: need immediate assistance.*

R & S flying together from the masthead means *crew has mutinied.*

The pirates' flag
In the 17th and 18th centuries pirates flew
a flag from their ship called the *Jolly Roger*,
which consisted of
a scull and two
crossed bones.

LIGHTS AT SEA

When shipping traffic greatly increased in the 19th century and collisions at night became a frequent occurrence, the British government developed a system of lights

to indicate the type of ship and its direction of travel. This system was then adopted internationally. The meanings of some of the lights are explained on the next pages.

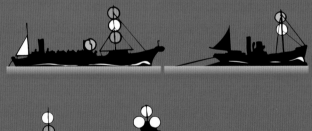

Motor boat less than 23 feet (7 m)
long, traveling at less than 7 knots

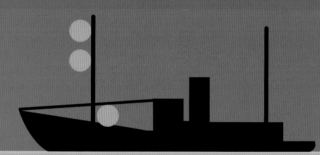

A vessel not under command

Vessel towing another

Sailing vessel
at anchor

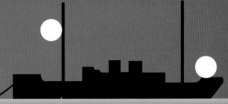

Vessel more than 148 feet
(45 m) long, at anchor

Sailing vessel
under way (viewed
from front)

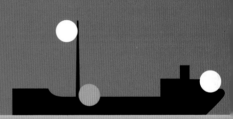

Steam vessel, less than 148 feet
(45 m) long, under way

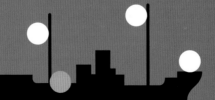

Steam vessel, more than 148 feet
(45 m) long under way

GROUND TO AIR

If you have to make a crash landing or bail out from an airplane in a remote area, you will need to communicate with rescuers in the air. Here are some internationally recognized signals that you can trample in snow or mark out with sticks, stones, cloth, or even pieces of plane wreckage.

Aircraft badly damaged

⌐_⌐

They are
deliberately very
simple shapes and
need to be made on a
very large scale to be
visible from the air.

211

Doctor required
(serious injuries)

Signal lamp
required

Medical supplies
required

Fuel and oil
required

All well

Not understood

Aircraft badly
damaged

Will attempt to
take off

Compass and
map required

Unable to proceed

Am proceeding in this direction

Probably safe to land here

Arms and ammunition required

Yes

No

Indicate direction and proceed

Food and water

Engineer required

ICHTHUS

The peoples of ancient India and Egypt knew the art of cryptography. The Israelites, too, enciphered words in their scriptures.

The followers of Jesus after the crucifixion also used a secret code sign. They had to help each other to survive. So the early Christians developed a code in the form of a fish sign. Greek was widely spoken at the time, and in that language *Iesous Christos Theou Uios Soter* means "Jesus Christ Son of God, Savior." If the initial letters of these words – *I*, *Ch*, *Th*, *U*, *S*, – are taken together they spell *ICHTHUS*, which is Greek for "fish."

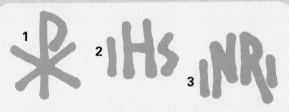

1 Chi Rho   The first two letters of Christ's name in Greek placed together

2 IHS   *Iesus Hominem Salvator* is Latin for "Jesus Savior of Men"

3 INRI   *Iesus Nazarenus Rex Iudaiorum* is Latin for "Jesus of Nazareth King of the Jews"

So the early Christians could draw a fish sign, or say the word ICHTHUS, to declare their faith secretly.

If you are about to form a secret society in your school, you could follow this method by making a secret sign from your initials.

1

SAINTLY SYMBOLS

In the Christian faith the founder and his followers were portrayed with symbols. Christ was symbolized by a lamb, cross, or both, as well as letters (see page 215).

The tellers of the story of Christ's life – the four evangelists Matthew, Mark, Luke, and John – each wrote an account called a gospel. Their symbols, along with those of Christ, have been used for 2,000 years in churches, manuscripts, paintings, and sculptures – wherever religious artists wished to convey the identity of the figures of early Christianity.

1 *Christ, a white lamb with halo and cross*
2 *Matthew, an angel*
3 *Mark, a winged lion*
4 *Luke, a winged ox*
5 *John, an eagle*

1 2 3 4 5 6

THE TWELVE APOSTLES

Nobody knows what the twelve men who worked with Jesus to teach the Christian faith actually looked like. Later illustrations in manuscripts, statues, and stained glass windows used symbols to portray them.

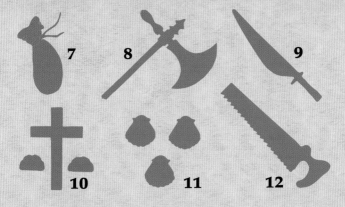

1. *Peter: the keys to the Kingdom of Heaven (usually crossed keys but sometimes one key only).*
2. *Andrew: decussate cross (he was crucified on a cross of this shape).*
3. *Thomas: spear or arrow ("doubting Thomas" thrust his hand into the wound made by a spear in Christ's side).*
4. *James the Less: a fuller's bat, a club used in the treatment of cloth.*
5. *John: chalice and dragon (or serpent).*
6. *Judas: club, cross, or sometimes a carpenter's square; often a boat.*
7. *Matthew: purse or money-box, sometimes a spear or ax.*
8. *Matthias: ax, halberd, lance, or sometimes a book and stone.*
9. *Bartholomew: butcher's flaying knife.*
10. *Philip: cross, often loaves and fishes.*
11. *James: scallop, shells.*
12. *Simon: a long saw, and sometimes one or two fish.*

TRAIL SIGNS

To right   *To left*   *Go left*   *Go right*

Trail signs were used by Native Americans to convey important or helpful information to future travelers passing along the trail. These signs were made from almost anything that was available in the local

FEATHER LANGUAGE

First kill   *Second battle*

To left   *To right*   *Three days to right*

area, such as knotted bunches of grass, small piles of stones, or sticks pushed into the ground. The freshness of the trail sign would let the travelers know how long ago the message had been posted.

Feathers were used by the Native Americans as a means of displaying to others what great deeds they had achieved in battle with other tribes.

I have killed an enemy

I have taken a scalp

I have been wounded

STONE SIGNS

Stone signs were like a secret code, visible only to the initiated. Trail signs disclosed their meaning only to an alert and experienced mind.

Over greater distances they communicated by smoke signals. One puff of smoke meant *attention*; two puffs meant *all's well*; three puffs, or three fires in a row, signified *danger*, *trouble*, or *a call for help*.

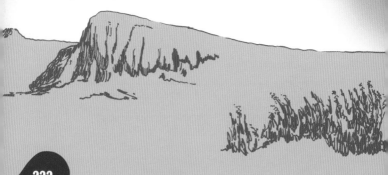

*Stone sign indicating direction
of stream or natural well*

223

QUIPU

During the 15th and 16th centuries the people called the Incas ruled one of the largest and richest civilizations in the Americas. The Incan empire covered much of today's Ecuador, Peru, Bolivia, Chile, and parts of Colombia and Argentina. The Incas' principal method of communication was called *quipu*. Since they didn't have horses or the wheel, they had to rely on runners to carry a series of knotted multicolored strings as messages.

CUSCO

A network of roads, based on two major north–south highways (about 2,000 miles long) linked the empire. About every 1.2 miles (2 km) along each of these roads there would be a small hut. These were rest stations for the runners who were responsible for carrying all government messages.

The messengers (*chasqui*) had a shell trumpet and wore a sun-bonnet of white feathers. Each runner worked for 15 days at a time. There were always between four and six men at each hut, depending on the importance of the task. They guaranteed the information was always sent at the fastest possible speed.

MAKE YOUR OWN QUIPU

If you want to make your own quipu you may start by stretching a cord of string between two chairs. You should use strings of different color to represent different classes of things.

You could, for instance, keep a record of your CDs, DVDs, tapes, and records. In case you have lots of them make sure you have some really long strings. As for the knots they will represent different things, depending on where you tie them. On the picture opposite the first string will keep a record of your CDs, and a single knot represents single units. Double twist knots are tens (second string), while hundreds have a piece of cloth tied into line.

CDs   DVDs   Tapes   Records

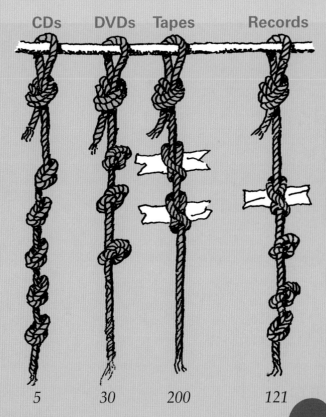

5   *30*   *200*   *121*

QUILT CODES

It is believed that in the early 1800s a quilt code was created in America to help slaves in the southern states to escape to freedom.

The code used several different quilting patterns. Linked together they would provide advice. The symbols sewn with patches of cloth onto blankets often derived from African cultures or were simple representations of everyday objects.

The finished quilts were hung over a washing line or in a window. In this way, the refugee slaves were able to find the escape route without drawing attention to themselves.

$1200 TO 1250 DOLLARS! FOR NEGROES!!

THE undersigned wishes to purchase a large lot of NEGROES for the New Orleans market. I will pay $1200 to $1250 for No. 1 young men, and $850 to $1000 for No. 1 young women. In fact I will pay more for likely

NEGROES,

Than any other trader in Kentucky. My office is adjoining the Broadway Hotel, on Broadway, Lexington, Ky., where I or my Agent can always be found.

WM. F. TALBOTT.

LEXINGTON, JULY 2, 1853.

Many slaves tried to escape to the northern states where they would be free. Traders offered rewards for captured slaves.

Follow the North Star code showed the way to those who traveled at night and were unfamiliar with the local landscape.

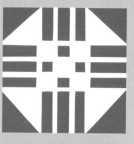

Follow the flying geese In spring geese migrate north, so following them in daytime led northwards.

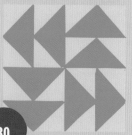

Get ready for the journey was a sign of a party gathering to escape together.

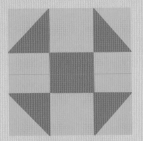

Meet at an agreed place was a sign that called together those who wished to escape.

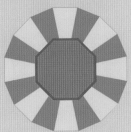

The wagon wheel Slaves sometimes hid in the false bottom of wagons going north.

Follow the bears' footprints In winter bears crossed the mountains and hills at the lowest passes.

If your enemy acquires the right information in time, he can easily win the war – a fact known to all military strategists since time immemorial. In ancient Greece, the Spartans knew how to send secret messages across

4

□□ JU
٦□U□

See pages 246–251 to work it out!

enemy lines. So did the United States in both World Wars. Warfare is a time when the secret languages of codes and ciphers flourish, and the side that is better at these activities wins the war.

THE SCYTALE

Four hundred years before the birth of Christ, some Greek soldiers were able to write secret messages.

They were Spartans and did not wish other Greeks to read what they had written.

Their secret code was written using a tool called a *scytale* – a cylindrical rod such as a spear or an ax handle. The successful transmission of messages depended on the sender and receiver having a scytale of the same diameter.

*Greek soldiers
decoding a message*

AN ANCIENT CIPHER

IAM · DEC ·

SATSNHA ·

IGRSEE ·

▼ This is a transposition cipher, where the letters are rearranged in an unfamiliar order.

▼ You can send messages to your friend if you both have a stick or tube – about 1–2 inches thick.

▼ The cardboard tube at the center of a roll of kitchen paper towels is ideal.

Two Greek warriors each with a spear.

▼ You will also need a length of paper to wrap around the stick. The best is a roll of adding machine paper bought at your local office supply store. You can, of course, cut your own ribbons.

▼ Begin by wrapping the strip around the tube in a spiral so that a narrow edge is exposed at each turn.

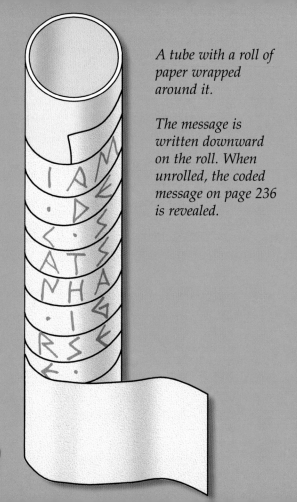

A tube with a roll of paper wrapped around it.

The message is written downward on the roll. When unrolled, the coded message on page 236 is revealed.

COMPLETING
YOUR CODE

▼ Then write your message along the edge of the roll, in even rows, writing downward.

▼ When the message is complete, you can unroll the tape and the letters will appear in a strange order that nobody else will be able to read.

▼ Your friend needs only to roll your strip around a cylinder of the same dimensions for the words to appear.

▼ If your friend does not have a roll, he can read this example by writing down the first letter, missing two, then noting the next letter or space mark, all the way through the message.

Benedict Arnold
(1741–1801)

Code betrayer Benedict Arnold , who was in charge of the West Point U.S. Military Academy, used a dictionary code message when he offered to betray West Point to the British during the American Revolution. In 1780 Arnold sent secret messages with a British Major, John André, to the attacking English army under the command of Sir Henry Clinton.

Arnold and Clinton both had copies of the same dictionary, and Arnold was able to select words from it and send the code numbers to the British, written on paper that was hidden in a boot. André was eventually captured, and the traitor Arnold had to escape the revolutionary army and join the British forces.

Benedict Arnold

90110-33129-1372

DICTIONARY CODE

Most people use a dictionary to find the meaning of a word. But you can also use a dictionary to create a secret code. You begin by being sure your friend has the same dictionary as you. Both should be the same edition, so that the words appear in exactly the same places.

▼ First write out your message:
I CAN READ THIS MESSAGE. Then find each word in the dictionary, and write down the page number, leaving a gap between each group.

  ▼ Next write 1 or 2 alongside the first numbers to indicate which column the word occurs in.

20-166220-109228

▼ Then count down the lines and write down that number.

▼ The word *CAN* occurs on page 33, 1st column, 29th line down.

▼ The great advantage when using this code is that only people with a copy of the same dictionary can decipher your message.

I	90110
CAN	33129
READ	137220
THIS	166220
MESSAGE	109228

words
hyp'nō-tīze, v., put into a trance-like state, -tism
hy'pō-, prefix, forms compounds with the meaning "beneath" or "under." Example:
hy-pō-dér'mic, n., injection under skin by needle

— I —

I, pro., first person singular
īce, n., frozen water
īce' crēam, n., frozen flavored cream
ich-thy-ol'ō-gy (ik-thi), n., science of fish
ī'ci-cle, n., long, sharp piece of ice
īc'ing, n., sugar frosting on cake
ī-con'ō-clast, n., image destroyer, attacker of conventional beliefs
ī'cy, a., frosty, frigid
ī-dē'à, n., imagined image, belief
ī-dē'ál-ly, adv., perfectly
ī-den'ti-cál, a., exact
ī-den'ti-fy, v., show as similar, recognize, -fication
ī-den'ti-ty, n., specific individuality
id-ē-ol'ō-gy, n., science of ideas and beliefs, -gical
id'i-öm, n., mode of expression, -atic
id-ī-ō-syn'crà-sy, n., unusual way of behavior, -tic
id'i-ōt, n., person with defective mentality, fool, -ic
ī'dle, a., unemployed, inactive
ī'dōl, n., worshipped image, hero, -atry
ī'dōl-īze, v., adore
if, conj., on condition, in case, although, whether
ig'lōō, n., Eskimo house of ice
ig-nīte', v., start fire, -nition
ig-nō'ble, a., low, unworthy
ig-nō-min'i-ous, a., shameful, disgraceful, -ly
ig'nō-rant, a., stupid

in fâre cär ǎll end

C
D

wood or metal
cam'bric, n., linen or cotton cloth, usually white
cam'el, n., one or two humped large ruminant animal
cá-mēl'lï-à (ya), n., shrub, flower
cá-mē'ō-pàrd, n., giraffe
cam'ē-ō, n., carved stone
cam'ēr-à, n., device for taking pictures
cam'i-sōle, n., garment worn under sheer top, woman's dressing gown
cam'ou-flàge (i-flàzh), v., disguise to deceive enemy
camp, n., place of campers
camp, v., live outdoors
cam-paign' (payn), n., military action, political competition
cam'phor (fèr), n., chemical for protecting clothing against moths, -ate
cam'pus, n., school grounds
campy, adj., in amusingly bad taste
can, v., be able to, know how, place food in cans
can, n., tin or metal container
cá-nal', artificial waterway -ize
can'á-pé (pay), n., small party sandwich
cá-nàrd', n., false rumor
cá-nár'y, n., yellow song bird
cá-nás'tà, n., card game
can'-can, n., kicking French high-dance
can'cél, v., wipe out, make void, -lation
can'cér, n., diseased malignant tumor growth, -ous
can-dē'-la (cd) n., unit of luminous intensity
can-dē-lā'brà, n., candlesticks
can-des'cént, n., a glowing
can'did, a., honest, outspoken, -ly
can'di-dāte, n., office seeker, dacy
can'died, a., sugar covered
can'dle, n., wax lighting device with wick, -r
can'dle, v., check eggs
can'dle-light, n., light by candle
can'dle-stick, n., candle holder

can'dōr, n., honesty, sincerity
can'dy, n., sugar confection
cāne, n., walking stick
cā'nīne, a., pertaining to dogs
can'is-tér, n., small metal container
can'kér, n., ulcerous sore, any decay
canned, a., sealed in can
can'nér-y, n., place for canning food
can'ni-bàl, n., person who eats human flesh, -ism
can'ning, n., preserving of food in cans
can'nōn, n., large gun firing heavy shells, -eer
can-nōn-āde', n., continuous firing
can'nōn-bàll, n., steel ball for cannon
can'ny, a., careful, shrewd
cá-noe' (new), n., light boat, -ist
can'ōn, n., law of church
can'ōn, n., clergyman attached to cathedral, -ical
can'ō-py, n., overhead covering
cant, n., insincere talk
can't, cont., can not
can-tā'bi-le (lay), a., flowing, song-like style
can'tá-lōupe, n., melon
can-tan'kér-ous, a., argumentative, -ly
cán-tā'tà (kèn-tàh-ta), n., story in song for chorus
can-tēēn', n., metal water container, military store
can'tér, n., slight gallop
can'ti-cle, n., religious chant
can'ti-lē-vér, n., projecting beam in architecture
can'til-lāte, v., chant, ation
can'tō, n., long poem
can-ton'ment, n., military camping place
can'tōr, n., traditional singer in synagogue
can'vàs, n., heavy woven cloth
can'vàs-back, n., type of duck
can'vàss, v., examine, seek for, solicit, -er
can'yōn, n., deep narrow valley
cap, n., cloth head covering
cá'pá-ble, a., having ability,

rod ōld wön fôr tōō good out oll owl pup ūnit ûrn

rav-i-o'li, *n.*, Italian dish

rav'ish, *v.*, carry off, enrapture, **-ing**

raw, *a.*, uncooked, raw

ray, *n.*, thin stream of light, line of invisible beams

ray'on, *n.*, synthetic fabric

rāze, *v.*, destroy

rā'zor, *n.*, shaving device

razz', *v.*, criticize lightly, heckle

rē- *prefix*, to do again

rēach, *v.*, touch, achieve, arrive

rē-act', *v.*, respond to, **-ion**

rē-ac'tion-ār-y, *n.*, extreme political conservative

rē-ac'tor, *n.*, device that produces atomic energy

rēad, *v.*, understand printed words, interpret

rēad'out, *n.*, display of information from computer, recorded by tape or typewriter

read'y (red), *a.*, prepared, prompt, at hand

read'y rōōm, *n.*, place where aircraft crews receive briefing and orders

rē'al, *a.*, actual, existing, **-ity**

rē'al-īze, *v.*, bring into existence, understand, profit, **-ization**

rē'al-ly, *adv.*, actually, in truth

realm (relm), *n.*, region, area of influence

rē'al tīme, *n.*, time in which occurrence and recording of an event are nearly simultaneous

rē'al-tor, *n.*, real estate broker

rēam, *n.*, 500 sheets of paper

rēap, *v.*, gather crop, receive results, **-er**

rēar, *n.*, end part, back, raise, bring up

rē'a'son (zuhn), *n.*, excuse for doing, motive, ability to think

rē'a'son-á-ble, *a.*, fair, sensible, reasonable

rē'a'son-ing, *n.*, thought behind actions

rē-as-sūre', *v.*, express faith in, **surance**

rē'bāte, *n.*, returned money

reb'el, *n.*, one who revolts, **-llion**

rē-bound', *v.*, bounce back

---

thiev'ér-y, *n.*, stealing

thīgh, *n.*, upper part of leg, femur

thim'ble, *n.*, finger protection while sewing

thin, *a.*, slender, slight, tenuous

thing, *n.*, object without life, event, single entity, item

think, *v.*, give mental image to, imagine, consider, **-ing**

think tank, *n.*, research group, institute

third, *a.*, after second

thirst, *n.*, craving for water, longing, **-y**

thir-tēen', *n.*, ten plus three, **-th**

thir'ty, *n.*, ten times three

this, *pro.*, thing near or present

this'tle, *n.*, plant with sharp points

thòrn, *n.*, sharp plant part, something causing distress or irritation

thòrn'y, *a.*, difficult, ticklish, having thorns

thòr'ough (-oh), *a.*, complete, exact

thòr'ough'bred, *n.*, pedigreed animal

thou, *pro.*, you

thōugh, *conj.*, despite, nevertheless

thōught, *n.*, thinking, reasoning, idea, opinion, consideration, mental process, **-ful**

thous'and, *n.*, ten times hundred, very large number

thrash, *v.*, beat, move about violently

thread, *n.*, fine cord, yarn, groove on screw

thread'bāre, *a.*, worn, shabby

threat, *n.*, promise of harm

threat'en, *v.*, portend, menace

thrēe, *n.*, cardinal numeral "3"

thresh, *v.*, remove grain from wheat, forge

thresh'ōld, *n.*, doorway, entrance, gate

thrift, *n.*, saving, frugality, management of money, **-y**

thrill, *n.*, excitement

thrill'êr, *n.*, mystery story

thrīve, *v.*, prosper, flourish, grow

---

relating to business

mêr'cè-nār-y, *a.*, interested only in money, greedy

mêr'chán-dīse, *n.*, articles bought and sold

mêr'chant, *n.*, one who operates store

mêr'cū-ry, *n.*, heavy chemical element

mêr'cy, *n.*, kindness, charity, clemency, **-ciful**

mēre, *a.*, only

mer-ē-trī'cious, *a.*, flashy, gaudy

merge (mèrj), *v.*, unite, combine, **-r**

mé-rid'i-án, *n.*, point in direct line with earth's poles

mer'it, *n.*, *v.*, value of, worth, virtue, deserve, earn

mer'ry, *a.*, full of fun, jolly, **-riment**

mesh, *n.*, net, network

mes'mer-īze, *v.*, hypnotize, fascinate

mess, *n.*, disorder, jumble, unpleasant situation, **-y**

mes'sāge, *n.*, written or spoken communication

mes'sén-gêr, *n.*, one who carries message

met'ál, *n.*, chemical element, *i.e.*: tin, iron, silver, etc., **-lic**

met-á-môr'phō-sis, *n.*, change in form

mē'tē-or, *n.*, particle in the solar system, **-ic**

mē'têr, *n.*, measuring machine, unit of length

meth'ōd, *n.*, way of accomplishing something, **-ic**

met'rō-nōme, *n.*, device for measuring musical time

met-rō-pol'ĭ-tán, *a.*, relating to a large city

met'tle (met-il), *n.*, courage, stamina

mez'zō (met-zō), *a.*, medium, moderate

mī-as'má (az), *n.*, poisonous mist

mī'crōbe, *n.*, minute living matter

mī'crō-film, *n.*, film used for recording, reduced printed material

mī'crō-phōne, *n.*, device which transmits sound

mī'crō-scōpe, *n.*, device that enlarges objects

mī-crō-scop'ic

L M

245

PIGPEN CIPHER

The American Civil War saw an old cipher becoming useful and popular again: the pigpen cipher, which goes back to the time of the Crusades of the 11th and 12th centuries.

The name of the cipher comes from the letters of the alphabet – the "pigs" – being trapped within the lines that form the "pens." The letters inside the "pens" are represented by the shapes made by these "pens," either with or without a dot.

You can set out the alphabet in any order you choose. Make sure your friend is using the same order. You can make two, three, or more copies, and give them to each of your friends so that all of you can send and receive messages.

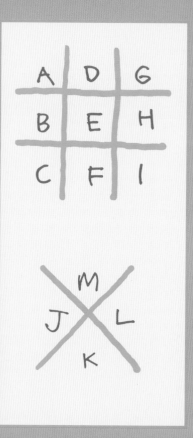

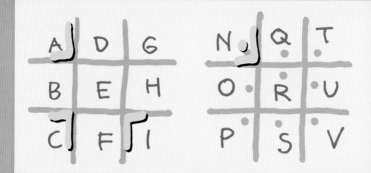

First write out your message

I CAN READ
THIS MESSAGE

Then write out the shapes of the pens that surround each letter, and add dots to those letters that are in the corners.

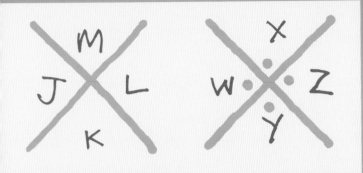

I CAN READ

Γ ᒥᒐ⅃ᒫ ᗷᗷ⅃∪

THIS MESSAGE

⅃ᑕᒥᗅ ∨ᗷᒐᒐᒐ⅃

Did you notice that there is a mistake in the drawing of the symbols? The dots from the two *S* letters in the word "message" are missing.

251

Albert James Myer
(1828–80)

A surgeon and U.S. Army officer, Albert
James Myer was the father of the Army
Signal Corps and its first chief signal
officer. Myer worked as a telegrapher
before studying medicine. He received his

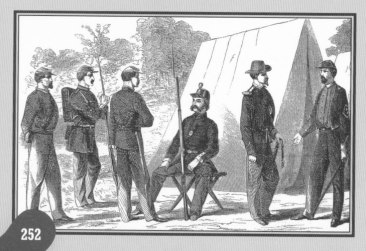

MD degree from Buffalo Medical College in 1851. His doctoral thesis, *A New Sign Language for Deaf Mutes*, used concepts he later found useful when devising aerial telegraphy. His major interest, besides medicine, was the invention of a system of signaling using simple codes and

Albert James Myer

lightweight materials. This system of codes used a single signal flag (or a lantern or kerosene torch at night) and was known as wigwag signaling or aerial telegraphy. It was adopted and used by both sides in the Civil War.

WIGWAG FLAGS

During the Civil War every signal officer was supposed to have a full signal set ready for use at all times. Signal equipment consisted of a kit, a canteen, and a haversack. The kit, or canvas signal case, contained the signal staff, flags, torch case, torches, and a wormer.

The Signal Corps used the wigwag flags to convey ideas by motions of a flag during the day or torch by night. Myer's system of wigwagging was made with four-element and two-element codes. The two codes are essentially identical.

There are two basic wigwag flags: one white with a red center, the other red with a white center. Only one wigwag flag was used at any one time.

THE FLAG MOVEMENTS

1 Brings the flag down on his right side

2 Brings the flag down on his left side

3 Brings the flag down in front of him

THE FLAG ALPHABET

Each letter had three flag waves:

A **112**	B **121**	C **211**	D **212**
E **221**	F **122**	G **123**	H **312**
I **213**	J **232**	K **323**	L **231**
M **132**	N **322**	O **223**	P **313**
Q **131**	R **331**	S **332**	T **133**
U **233**	V **222**	W **311**	X **321**
Y **111**	Z **113**		

CHOCTAW TALK

Fourteen Choctaw Indian men were recognized as the first to use their native language as an unbreakable code in World War I. Toward the end of the war, they helped the American Expeditionary Force win several key battles in the Meuse-Argonne campaign in France against the Germans. With at least one

Choctaw man placed in each field company headquarters, they communicated by field telephone, translated radio messages into the Choctaw language, and wrote field orders. The German army, which captured about one in four messengers, never deciphered the messages written in Choctaw.

THE CODE TALKERS

The Navajo people are the
largest tribe of Native Americans.
They live in the southwest
states of Arizona,
Utah, and New
Mexico. Until recently
their language, which has no alphabet
or symbols, had never been written down.
In describing their language, speakers
often say that spoken words paint
pictures in their minds.

INTO BATTLE

World War II presented the U.S. military with the problem of how to make secret messages that their enemies couldn't break. They came up with the idea of recruiting the Navajo people.

The Navajo recruits became the famous Code Talkers who were given the task of transmitting information on tactics, troop movements, orders, and other crucial battlefield information via telegraphs and radios in their native tongue. A major advantage of the code talker system was its speed. Morse code often took hours whereas the Navajos handled a message in minutes. The Navajos' spoken language was understood by fewer than 30 non-Navajos at the time. The complexity of the language made the code extremely difficult for anyone else to decipher.

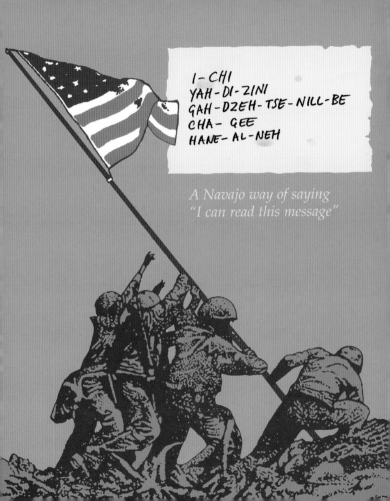

I-CHI
YAH-DI-ZINI
GAH-DZEH-TSE-NILL-BE
CHA-GEE
HANE-AL-NEH

*A Navajo way of saying
"I can read this message"*

ENIGMA

The Enigma encryption machines were first developed in Germany in the 1920s, but they did not become widely used until World War II, when they were essential to the Nazi war effort.

The Nazis believed Enigma was the most secure cipher system ever built, and it was. It used a combination of wired rotors and plugs to change, or encrypt, each letter as it was pressed on the keyboard. Every day, the order of the wired rotors inside the machine was changed according to a keylist. In this way, an enemy couldn't figure out its complicated pattern.

But the creation of the Navy Bombe spelled the death sentence for the security of Enigma's messages.

An Enigma encryption machine

Klappe
schliessen

ENIGMA

THE NAVY BOMBE

At the beginning of the 1930s, Polish mathematicians made the first attempts at "breaking" the Enigma code.

After many years of trying, they finally discovered how the encryptions were made. The problem was that the Enigma's key was changed every day. Breaking Germany's secret messages by hand was too slow. And that was why they created the Bombe to test the Enigma's 17,576 settings.

The Germans made improvements on the Enigma as World War II continued. Fortunately, the U.S. Navy, working with the National Cash Register Company, built U.S. Navy Cryptanalytic Bombes to break the Nazis' secret messages. This helped the Allies to win the war in Europe.

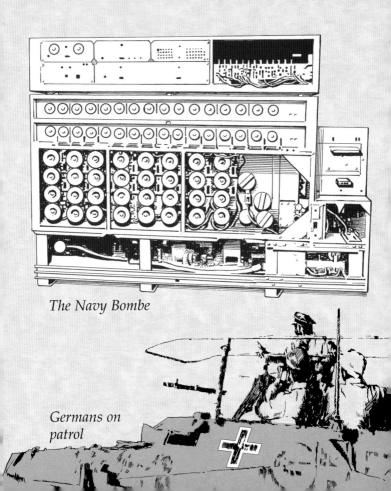

The Navy Bombe

Germans on patrol

PURPLE, CORAL,

イケネラ

During World War II, the Japanese cipher machines were called PURPLE, CORAL, and JADE. All three machines were built from common telephone stepping switches. JADE was different from CORAL and PURPLE in that it enciphered messages in *katakana*, using an alphabet of 50 symbols. Katakana are a syllabary, one of four Japanese writing systems. The others are *hiragana*, *kanji*, and *rōmaji*. The word

AND JADE

ダメシゲ

katakana means "partial kana." Katakana are characterized by short straight strokes and angular corners and are the simplest of the Japanese scripts.

KATAKANA

ア a	カ ka	サ sa	タ ta	ナ na	ハ ha	マ ma	ヤ ya
イ i	キ ki	シ shi	チ chi	ニ ni	ヒ hi	ミ mi	
ウ u	ク ku	ス su	ツ tsu	ヌ nu	フ fu	ム mu	ユ yu
エ e	ケ ke	セ se	テ te	ネ ne	ヘ he	メ me	
オ o	コ ko	ソ so	ト to	ノ no	ホ ho	モ mo	ヨ yo

i can read

イ ケ ネ ラ ダ
i ke ne ra da

ALPHABET

ラ ra	ワ wa		ガ ga	ザ za	ダ da	バ ba	パ pa
リ ri			ギ gi	ジ ji	ヂ ji	ビ bi	ピ pi
ル ru			グ gu	ズ zu	ヅ zu	ブ bu	プ pu
レ re			ゲ ge	ゼ ze	デ de	ベ be	ペ pe
ロ ro	ヲ o	ン n	ゴ go	ゾ zo	ド do	ボ bo	ポ po

message

me   shi   ge

GLOSSARY

Anagram A word, phrase, or sentence changed by transposing its letters. Thus *are* is an anagram for "ear."

Autokey An encryption key that changes with each communication.

Character A letter, figure, punctuation mark, or other symbol used in writing or printing.

Cipher A method or system of changing text to hide its real meaning where each letter is changed to something else. For example: A=*F* or A=** or A=£

Cipher alphabet A table that shows what each letter is replaced with. For example: A=*B*, B=*C* , C=*D*, etc.

Code A system of changing entire words or phrases into something else. For example: President = *Eagle* or *Battleship* = *13425*

Codebook A book or other document that lists the answers (the key) to a secret code.

Codebreaker A person who uses cryptanalysis to solve secret codes and ciphers without having the key.

Codemaker A person who makes new secret codes and ciphers.

Coral A Japanese cipher machine during World War II.

Crib A method of codebreaking that uses part of the assumed (guessed) plaintext to compare against the cipher.

Cryptanalysis The area of cryptology that deals with the study of a secret message or a group of secret messages and breaking the system so you can read what it says without first knowing the key.

Cryptogram A message that has been written in a secret cipher.

Cryptography The area of cryptology that deals with making codes or cipher systems so that others cannot read what is in the secret message.

Cryptologist A person who makes and/or breaks codes.

Cryptology The art and science of making (cryptography) and breaking (cryptanalysis) codes.

Cryptosystem A method or process of encryption or decryption.

Decipher To change a secret encoded message back to the real plaintext so you can read it. To *decode* or *decrypt* is the same as to decipher!

Encipher To use a secret system to change a message into a secret that only you and your friends know how to read.

To *encode* or *encrypt* is the same as to encipher!

Encryption A general term for enciphering or coding.

Enigma The name of a machine used by the Germans to encrypt and decrypt secret messages in World War II.

Grid A network of uniformly spaced horizontal and perpendicular lines.

Hieroglyphic A system of writing in mainly pictorial characters.

Homophone A cipher that translates a single plaintext character into any one of multiple ciphertext characters that all have the same meaning.

Intelligence Information about an enemy that has been studied for its importance and accuracy and is provided to warfighters and decision-makers.

Jade Codename for machine used by the Japanese Imperial Navy to encrypt and decrypt messages during World War II.

Key A symbol or group of symbols used for controlling the making (cryptography) and breaking (cryptanalysis) of codes. For example: If your key is A=*X*, B=*Y*, C=*Z*, both you and your friends need to know that to encrypt and decrypt the message.

Matrix A rectangular arrangement of characters into rows or columns.

Mudra Symbolic Indian hand gestures used in religious ceremonies, dances, and yoga.

Nomenclator A collection of syllables, words, and names with a separate cipher alphabet.

Null Meaningless numbers, letters, or symbols used to complete a group or fill out a pattern, making decryption more difficult.

Plaintext A message written in regular characters readable by all without any hidden or secret meaning.

Polyalphabetic Using more than one alphabet.

Purple Codename for the Japanese system of encrypting diplomatic messages during World War II.

Recovery The process of figuring out a code or key by studying (cryptanalysis) the message or messages.

Semaphore A communications systems where hand-held flags or mechanical arms are moved into different positions to convey messages to an observer.

Setting The position of parts of a cryptosystem or cipher machine, like a starting point. For example: The Germans needed to set the ENIGMA machine to the right rotor setting before beginning to encrypt or decrypt their messages during World War II.

Sign language A visual means of communication using physical gestures instead of words.

Slide The number of position changes between the plaintext and the encoded text. For example,

Plaintext:
ABCDEFGHIJKLMNOPQRSTUVWXYZ
Enciphered text:
VWXYZABCDEFGHIJKLMNOPQRSTU
Slide: 5

Substitution cipher A method of encrypting a message where the characters of the plaintext are in the same order but are switched to other characters.
For example: A=*D*, B=*E*, C=*F*, etc.

Transposition cipher A method of encrypting a message where the character positions are changed but the characters themselves stay the same. For example,
SECRETS = *ECTSRES*

TEXTING

Just about anybody with a cell phone will have sent or received a text message. To speed up communication with these messages, a system of shorthand has evolved that utilizes many techniques of abbreviation. One of these involves substituting numbers for similar sounds in words: for example, *L8* means "late" and *2MORO*, "tomorrow." This is also done with letters, for example *C U B4 2NITE* would mean "see you before tonight." Another technique is to drop the vowels from a word: for example, *RGDS* means "regards." One other method is to use just the initials from a well-known phrase such as "in my humble opinion" – IMHO.

Some text message abbreviations

AFAIK "as far as I know"
ATB "all the best"
BCNU "be seeing you"
CID "consider it done"
D8 "date"
EZ "easy"
FWIW "for what it's worth"
GR8 "great"
LOL "laughing out loud" or "lots of love"
MYOB "mind your own business"
NE "any"
OTOH "on the other hand"
PCM "please call me"
prolly "probably"
SRY "sorry"
THNQ "thank you"
W8 "wait"
XLNT "excellent"
YR "your"

KOOB SIHT YOJNE UOY DID

BACK SLANG

The most popular code used by young people is to speak the words of a sentence backward.

Can you read the message at the top of this page?

Did you enjoy this book?

Take any simple sentence and practice saying it backward.

*KOOB SIHT DEYOJNE
UOY EPOH EW*

283

INDEX